D0528310

low cost
cooking

Wendy Godfrey

SIMON & SCHUSTER
A VIACOM COMPANY

First published in Great Britain by Simon & Schuster, 1999
A Viacom Company

Copyright © 1999, Weight Watchers International, Inc.

Simon & Schuster UK Ltd
Africa House
64-78 Kingsway
London WC2B 6SX

Weight Watchers and 1, 2, 3 Success 2000 are Trademarks of Weight Watchers International, Inc.
and used under its control by Weight Watchers (UK) Ltd.

Design: Moore Lowenhoff
Cover design: Jane Humphrey
Typesetting: Stylize Digital Artwork
Photography: Steve Lee
Styling: Marian Price
Food preparation: Sian Davies

Weight Watchers Publications Manager: Elizabeth Egan
Weight Watchers Publications Assistant: Celia Whiston

A CIP catalogue record is available from the British Library

ISBN: 0 85941 969 X

Printed in Hong Kong

Pictured on the front cover: *Garlicky Baked Potato and Quick Onion Baked Bean Pizza (page 34)*

Pictured on the back cover: *Apple Snow and Double Orange Dessert (page 75)*

Recipe notes:
Egg size is medium, unless otherwise stated.
Fruit and vegetables are medium-sized, unless otherwise stated.
It is important to use proper measuring spoons, not cutlery, for spoon measures.
1 tablespoon = 15 ml; 1 teaspoon = 5 ml.
Dried herbs can be substituted for fresh ones, but the flavour may not always
be as good. Halve the fresh herb quantity stated in the recipe.

Ⓥ shows the recipe is suitable for vegetarians.

Contents

Introduction

Everyone needs to cut the cost of their housekeeping at some time, whether it's after Christmas, when extra bills have to be paid or when you are planning some other major purchase which means a cut in other parts of the family finances. Many of us need to count the pennies generally, but this does not mean that we have to eat poorly or cook food with little taste. Careful shopping and an awareness of what can be bought cheaply, and where and when to shop for cheaper food of all kinds, can cut the bills quite drastically.

In this book, you will find recipes which cost very little to make. I am reluctant to put a price limit on the dishes as many foods vary in price seasonally, particularly fresh fruit and vegetables – compare the price of raspberries in midsummer and then look at the price of them, if you dare, just before Christmas. I have tried to make the ingredients 'stretch' and to use every part of the food, therefore avoiding waste. For example, broccoli stalks are used to make delicious Broccoli Soup (page 11), leaving the florets for other dishes, such as Lemon Rice with Seasonal Vegetables (page 37) and Broccoli, Mushroom and Sweetcorn Pizza (page 41); a chicken is casseroled (Greek Lemon Chicken, page 59) and, after the meat is removed, the carcass is used for soup stock. The dishes are suitable for everyone in the household, whether a Weight Watchers Member or not, and serving ideas are given for bulking the meal out, for those who are not trying to lose weight.

Shopping Economically

It is essential to set a weekly budget for food. This makes sense even if you aren't counting the pennies, but is even more important when economy is of the essence.

One of the best ways of economising is to buy foods, particularly fresh vegetables and fruit, when they are in season; for example, root and green leafy vegetables and citrus fruit in winter and soft fruit and salads in summer. It is now easy to buy fruits like strawberries all the year round, but compare the prices of the traditional British ones in June with those bought at other times of the year and you will see what I mean about seasonality and economy.

Most food shoppers will know that the cheapest basic foods are the starchy ones, such as potatoes, pasta, rice, beans and flour. Recipes using these basics in an imaginative way will feature strongly in this book.

Small quantities of meat have been used in some recipes but only the less expensive cuts; in the recipes using fish, only the cheaper varieties or canned fish feature as the main ingredient.

Convenience foods can often save money. Canned beans in all their varieties, for example, are ready to cook without the need for tedious pre-soaking and long cooking, thus saving fuel, and come in manageable quantities. Frozen foods can often be economical and time-saving. Some frozen, ready-prepared vegetables such as sliced onions and casserole mixes mean that a meal can be ready in minutes just by taking one or two spoonfuls out of the bag. Frozen peas can cost very little and look better than canned peas on the plate. Another bonus is that very little nutritional value is lost in the freezing process. Shaved cold meats are good for sandwiches and salads. They are ideal when you are trying to lose weight because they are cut so thin and can be bulked out with low-calorie fresh vegetables. Some pizza bases can be kept in the store cupboard without the need for chilling and freezing and make a good base for low-calorie and low-fat toppings. Skimmed milk powder is not only a useful standby for those days when you suddenly run out of milk, but milk made from powder is an ideal ingredient in sauces and puddings.

Look out for special offers but assess whether they really are a bargain for you; for example, can you really use all of a large or multiple pack before it reaches its 'best before' date?, is it something that can be stored in the correct conditions at home?

When shopping, read the nutritional labels, which are found on almost all packaged goods. You will know from your Weight Watchers information what to look out for – foods which are mainly low in fat – for example, canned tuna in water is much better for Weight Watchers Members than canned tuna in oil; low sugar and salt-free baked beans are better than the regular beans.

A time of economy is not the time to experiment wildly with unusual ingredients, just in case they are not liked. Keep to the familiar, but perhaps try a different combination of dishes or combine familiar ingredients in a new way, for a change. If you like pasta and you like beans, you will love Bean and Pasta Soup (page 19). Look out for the ideas given as alternatives at the end of a recipe. This may be something that you would like but haven't previously thought of.

I have made use of the cuisines of countries where economy is always the watchword. Indian food is now familiar here and uses many inexpensive ingredients. Southern-Italian food makes the most of home-grown ingredients and uses very little meat. Fish is plentiful there, as nowhere is far from the coast. The cooking of the Middle East, with its grains and spices, is also a source of inspiration.

Low-Cost Cooking

Besides the cost of food itself, another major consideration is the cost of fuel for cooking. Raw foods, like salads, are ideal as no cooking is involved and nearly all of the nutrients are retained. There are, however, times when the comfort of something warming is needed and a salad will not do.

A microwave cooker uses far less electricity than a conventional cooker so, where this is a good means of cooking something, it is mentioned in the method as an alternative. Ovens use the most fuel of any method, so economical use of the oven when it has to be switched on is emphasised in these recipes, for example, accompaniments to serve with a baked dish can often be baked alongside it. You can also economise by making two or three loaves of bread or pizzas and so on, at the same time, and freezing the others for future use.

Steaming is a quicker method of cooking than boiling and retains more nutrients in vegetables. It is often possible to steam vegetables or potatoes in a metal colander or sieve over a pan in which your main course is cooking, thus eliminating the need for heating two rings. Vegetable Couscous (page 41) makes use of this idea.

Some small pieces of cooking equipment can aid economy, for example, pressure cookers cook all kinds of foods, in a fraction of the normal time, thus saving fuel. Conversely, slow-cookers cook food very gently and slowly but save fuel by using a very small amount of power. Both are especially good for casseroles; a non-stick pan can be used for stir-fries and other vegetable cooking, with the need for little oil, and heavy-based pans retain heat evenly and well, allowing you to set the cooking heat lower than otherwise. Tiered steamers make it possible to cook several different components of a meal, such as a casserole, potatoes and vegetables, on the heat from one ring.

Other Economical Hints

Even with a small garden (or no garden at all!), some foods can be grown at home in pots or window boxes. The most successful of these to grow are herbs and salads, which can make all the difference to the flavour of dishes. If you do have a garden, digging is a good weight-losing exercise!

There are many foods to be had for free. Blackberries are the hedgerow fruits which spring to mind most readily and field mushrooms are available at much the same time of year (but do take care only to gather mushrooms you know are edible). Windfalls of apples and pears are readily given away by people who have fruit trees in their gardens. If you know a fisherman, he may be willing to share his catch.

'Pick Your Own' farms are now established as an economical way to get fruit and vegetables in season and the exercise in fresh air is good for you, too.

Some towns and villages have markets in which local produce is sold. It is always best to go to a trusted stallholder, though, as the fruit and vegetables are sometimes past their best and it will be a false economy to buy them if you end up throwing away a large proportion.

Joining a food co-operative to buy in bulk cheaply and share the costs sometimes works well. You must get on well with the others in the group and have rules for payment and the division of goods.

Most people shop in supermarkets, so look out for their special offers and also their display of slightly-less-than-perfect goods. If there is something there that you use regularly, it is worth buying at the lower price.

Good Cooking!

Soups

The 'soup kitchen' is aptly named. If there is one group of dishes where it is possible to economise, this is it.

Most of these recipes use stock as the main liquid. You can, of course, use ready-made stock cubes and boiling water, but do think of alternatives. Any vegetable water can be used as stock, so don't drain the vegetables down the sink. Put the liquid in a jug or plastic container. If you have roasted a chicken, don't put the carcass in the bin. Cook it, covered with water and with a carrot and an onion, herbs and some salt and pepper. Another inexpensive source of stock is to ask the butcher for a bacon hock bone. These often come with some meat on them, which can be minced and used in one of the meat recipes, and the ham stock is ideal for Split-Pea and Ham Soup (page 16). Remember that the chicken and ham stocks are not suitable for vegetarians, though.

For main ingredients, always use what is in season. Sometimes, vegetables which are past their best can be disguised in a soup. I often make a 'refrigerator' soup, with any items that need to be used up in the fridge, which I liven up with a squeeze of tomato purée and thicken with a handful of small pasta. This is what the Italians do when they are making minestrone – using seasonal vegetables and pasta.

Most soups can be frozen. As most of the recipes are for four servings, it may be most useful to do this in individual portions, so that you can have a quick lunch or snack, with a little bread, if Points permit. Yogurt or cottage-cheese cartons are useful for freezing single portions of soup.

Celeriac and Apple Soup

Serves: 4

Preparation time: 10 minutes + 25–30 minutes cooking
Calories per serving: 35

Freezing: recommended

Ⓥ

The apple adds a sharpness to this soup. Use the other half of the celeriac in Celeriac and Herb Salad (page 27), or as one of the vegetables in Vegetable Couscous (page 41).

1 onion, chopped
850 ml (1½ pints) vegetable stock
1 teaspoon curry powder or paste (optional)
250 g (9 oz) celeriac (about half a standard size), cut into 1 cm (½-inch) cubes
1 large cooking apple, peeled, cored and cut into quarters
chopped fresh parsley, to garnish

1. Put the onion in a large pan, with enough stock or water to cover and the curry powder or paste, if used. Cover the pan and simmer for 5 minutes.
2. Add the celeriac and the remaining stock and cook, covered, for a further 15 minutes.
3. Add the apple and cook for a further 5 minutes, until the apple has collapsed.
4. Either mash the soup with a potato masher or liquidise it in a food processor or liquidiser.
5. Serve sprinkled with parsley.

Weight Watchers note:
Some fresh wholemeal bread would go well with this soup, if Points permit.

Points per serving: ½
Total Points per recipe: 2

Broccoli Soup

Serves: 4

Preparation time: 10 minutes
+ 20 minutes cooking
Calories per serving: 50

Freezing: not recommended

Ⓥ

Some people throw away the thick stem at the base of the broccoli but there is plenty of flavour there and it makes a delicious, delicately coloured soup. Save the rest of the broccoli for Broccoli, Mushroom and Sweetcorn Pizza (page 41), or for one of the dishes using seasonal vegetables.

1 onion
850 ml (1½ pints) vegetable stock
1 trimmed broccoli stem, chopped coarsely
1 potato, weighing about 100 g (3½ oz), peeled and chopped coarsely
salt and freshly ground black pepper

1. Grate the onion or chop it coarsely. Put it in a pan, with 150 ml (¼ pint) of vegetable stock. Bring to the boil and simmer for 5 minutes.
2. Add the broccoli and the potato and stir well. Add the remainder of the stock, bring to the boil and simmer for 15 minutes.
3. Mash well with a potato masher or liquidise the soup. Season to taste, with salt and pepper.

Points per serving: ½
Total Points per recipe: 1

Chicken and Tomato Soup

Serves: 4

Preparation time: 15 minutes
+ 25 minutes cooking
Calories per serving: 55

Freezing: recommended

Ⓥ

Although there is one chicken thigh in the ingredients list, you could use the stock from a chicken carcass (see chapter introduction) instead, taking as much meat off it as possible, which will cut down on the cost. Canned tomatoes are often on special offer.

1 onion, chopped
1 medium boneless and skinless chicken thigh, cut into strips
850 ml (1½ pints) water or chicken stock
400 g (14 oz) canned tomatoes
1 tablespoon tomato purée
1 teaspoon sugar (optional)
salt and freshly ground black pepper

1. Put the onion and chicken in a large pan, with about 6 tablespoons of the water or stock. Cover and simmer for 5 minutes, until the onion has softened and the chicken has turned white.
2. Add the tomatoes, tomato purée and remaining stock. Bring to the boil and simmer for 20 minutes.
3. If canned whole tomatoes have been used, mash with a wooden spoon or potato masher to break them up.
4. Season to taste with salt and pepper. If the soup tastes sharp, the addition of the sugar will remedy this.

Cook's note:
The soup can be frozen in individual portions. Yogurt or cottage cheese pots are ideal for this; cover them in foil or use the plastic lid.

Points per serving: 1
Total Points per recipe: 3

Tandoori Parsnip Soup

Serves: 4

Preparation time: 10 minutes
+ 20 minutes cooking
Calories per serving: 70

Freezing: recommended

Ⓥ

The flavour of curry and parsnips go particularly well together. Although a tandoori spice mix adds the best flavour, any curry powder or paste of your choice will do.

1 onion, chopped
850 ml (1½ pints) water or vegetable stock
2 teaspoons tandoori paste or other curry paste or powder
250 g (9 oz) parsnips, chopped roughly
25 g (1 oz) long-grain rice
salt and freshly ground black pepper

1. Put the onion in a pan, with 3 tablespoons of the water or stock and the curry paste or powder. Cover and simmer for 3 or 4 minutes.
2. Add the remaining water or stock, the parsnips and the rice. Bring to the boil and then simmer for 15 minutes, or until the parsnips and rice grains are tender.
3. Either mash, to make chunky soup, or liquidise, to make a smoother soup.
4. Season to taste – you probably won't need pepper.

Weight Watchers note:
If Points permit, some Indian bread would be a good accompaniment. This is now widely available in supermarkets and in Indian stores. Buy it on special offer and freeze it.

Points per serving: ½
Total Points per recipe: if using tandoori paste 4½; if not 3½

Chilled Lemon Soup

Serves: 4

Preparation time: 10 minutes
+ 15 minutes cooking + chilling
Calories per serving: 45

Freezing: not recommended

Ⓥ

This is a refreshing soup when the weather is hot. Lemons are at their cheapest in the winter, however, and this soup can be eaten hot, too.

1 small onion, chopped finely
1 tablespoon cornflour
1 large lemon
425 ml (¾ pint) vegetable stock
150 ml (¼ pint) skimmed milk
salt and freshly ground black pepper
4 tablespoons low-fat plain fromage frais, to serve

1. Put the onion in a pan, with 3 tablespoons of water, cover and heat slowly for 5 minutes, until the onion is soft.
2. Blend the cornflour in 1 tablespoon of water and stir in. Thinly peel the zest of half the lemon with a peeler and add to the pan. Grate the other half of the lemon peel and reserve for garnish. Gradually blend in the stock and milk.
3. Bring to the boil and simmer for a few minutes.
4. Squeeze the juice from the lemon and add to the soup. Allow to cool and then chill. (If serving hot, strain and reheat and serve at once.)
5. Strain when cold. Season to taste and serve with a tablespoon of fromage frais in each bowl and a sprinkling of the reserved grated lemon zest.

Variation:
This soup is delicious when made with home-made chicken stock. This does, of course, make it unsuitable for vegetarians.

Points per serving: 1½
Total Points per recipe: 5½

Carrot and Ginger Soup

Serves: 4

Preparation time: 5 minutes
+ 20–25 minutes cooking
Calories per serving: 60

Freezing: recommended

(v)

1 onion, chopped
1 teaspoon ground ginger
850 ml (1½ pints) vegetable
  stock
350 g (12 oz) carrots, sliced
15 g (½ oz) soup pasta (very
  tiny shapes)
salt and freshly ground black
  pepper

**Carrots have a pronounced
flavour which is superb with
ginger. The small pasta that
looks like rice works well but,
if you have children in the
house, they might like the
'alphabet soup' pasta in this
colourful orange soup.**

1. Heat the onion and ginger in a covered pan, with about 6 tablespoons of the stock.
2. Add the sliced carrots when the onion looks soft.
3. Pour in the remaining stock and bring to the boil. Turn down to a simmer and cook, covered, for about 20 minutes.
4. Either mash the soup with a potato masher or liquidise it.
5. Add the pasta and season to taste with salt and pepper.
6. Heat through for another 5 minutes, until the pasta is soft.

Variations:
Use a little grated fresh root ginger instead of the ground ginger. This will give a sharper flavour.
  Use parsnips instead of carrots, adding an extra 3½ Points per recipe and 1 Point per serving.

Cook's note:
One of the pieces of kitchen equipment I find most useful is a hand-held electric liquidiser. It is superb for soups, as all the blending can be done in the pan, and it is very easy to wash.

Points per serving: 0
Total Points per recipe: 0

Moroccan Lentil Soup

Serves: 4

Preparation time: 5 minutes
+ 1 hour cooking
Calories per serving: 155

Freezing: recommended

(v)

1 onion, chopped
1 teaspoon each ground
  cinnamon, turmeric and
  paprika
1.2 litres (2 pints) water
1 small courgette, (sliced
  thinly)
175 g (6 oz) red lentils
200 g (7 oz) canned tomatoes
1 tablespoon chopped fresh
  mint
salt

**The flavours and colours of
Morocco are warm and this
soup is typically Moroccan.
Although it takes a long time
to cook, once the heat has
been turned down to a simmer,
the soup can be left without
supervision.**

1. Put the chopped onion and the spices in a pan, with 4 tablespoons of the water, cover and cook gently for about 5 minutes, until the onion is soft.
2. Add the courgette, the lentils, the canned tomatoes and the remaining water.
3. Bring to the boil and then turn down to a simmer. Cover and cook for 45 minutes–1 hour.
4. Season to taste with salt and stir in the mint just before serving.

Cook's note:
For a more substantial soup, add half a 432 g can of chick-peas with the lentils, which increases the Points to 1½ Points per serving and 6 Points per recipe. Mash the soup down at the end of the cooking time, to break down the chick-peas. Use the other half of the can in Chick-pea Dip with Raw Vegetables (page 27) or in a salad.

Points per serving: ½
Total Points per recipe: 2½

Onion Broth

Serves: 4

Preparation time: 10 minutes + 1 hour cooking
Calories per serving: 55

Freezing: recommended

V

The reason this soup takes so long to cook is the addition of pearl barley, a traditional broth ingredient. You could make something similar in half the time by using rice or small pasta instead, or the soup could be cooked more quickly in a pressure cooker.

2 onions, chopped
1 leek, sliced (optional)
1.2 litres (2 pints) vegetable stock
2 tablespoons pearl barley
1 tablespoon chopped fresh parsley
salt and freshly ground black pepper

1. Put the onions and the leek in a pan, with 6 tablespoons of the stock. Cover and simmer for 5 minutes, or until the onions are soft.
2. Add the remaining stock and pearl barley. Bring to the boil, cover and simmer for just under an hour.
3. Just before serving, add the parsley and season to taste with salt and pepper.

Points per serving: $\frac{1}{2}$
Total Points per recipe: 2

Split-pea and Ham Soup

Serves: 4

Preparation time: overnight soaking + 10 minutes + 1 hour cooking
Calories per serving: 230

Freezing: recommended

This is almost a main meal – a real 'rib-sticker' – but still good for Weight Watchers Members. If you have a butcher who sells ham on the bone, ask him if you can buy the bone. Very often, he will almost give it away.

225 g (8 oz) green or yellow split-peas
1.5 litres ($2\frac{3}{4}$ pints) water
1 ham bone or hock
1 onion, chopped
1 large potato, peeled and cut into small cubes
1 tablespoon chopped fresh parsley
freshly ground black pepper

1. Soak the split-peas in half the water, overnight.
2. Put them and their soaking water along with the remaining water in a large pan, with the ham bone, the onion and the potato. Bring to the boil and then simmer for 50 minutes.
3. Remove the bone and scrape any meat left on it into the pan.
4. Season to taste with pepper only, because the ham is naturally salty and will have flavoured the soup already.
5. Stir in the chopped parsley.
6. If you like a less chunky soup, mash the contents of the pan with a potato masher.

Variations:
Use red lentils instead of the split peas.
For a more oniony flavour, add chopped spring onions or chives instead of the parsley.

Points per serving: 3
Total Points per recipe: 13

Chilled Marrow and Mint Soup

Serves: 4

Preparation time: 15 minutes
+ 20 minutes cooking
Calories per serving: 100

Freezing: recommended

Ⓥ

Marrow often seems to be a tasteless vegetable but here the mint adds a delicious flavour and the marrow's texture is just right for a chilled soup. This soup can, of course, be eaten hot as well.

1 kg (2 lb 4 oz) marrow
1 tablespoon oil
300 ml (1/2 pint) skimmed milk
600 ml (1 pint) well-flavoured vegetable stock
1 tablespoon cornflour
1 tablespoon chopped fresh mint
salt and freshly ground black pepper

1. Peel the marrow and remove and discard the seeds. Cut into chunks.
2. Put in a pan and cover with cold water. Bring to the boil and immediately drain. This will help to preserve the green colour of the marrow.
3. In the same pan, heat the oil and add the marrow and some salt and pepper. Cover and simmer gently for 10 minutes, or until the marrow is soft.
4. Add the milk and the stock and bring to the boil.
5. Remove the pan from the heat and mash the soup with a potato masher or rub through a sieve.
6. Blend the cornflour with a little water and add to the soup. Bring to the boil again.
7. If serving cold, leave the soup in the pan, with the lid on, until cold (you could plunge the base of the pan into cold water, to speed up the process) and then chill. Stir in the mint just before serving. Taste and adjust the seasoning. If serving hot, add the mint and adjust the seasoning.

Variation:
Instead of marrow, use any of the marrow family, such as squashes, cucumber or courgettes.

Points per serving: 1
Total Points per recipe: 4 1/2

Bean and Pasta Soup

Serves: 4

Preparation time: 10 minutes
+ 30 minutes cooking
Calories per serving: 145

Freezing: recommended

Ⓥ

A really filling winter soup, but without lots of Calories. Use any combination of beans and pasta shapes.

1 onion, chopped
1 carrot, chopped
850 ml (1 1/2 pints) vegetable stock
100 g (3 1/2 oz) pasta shapes
200 g (7 oz) canned red kidney beans, drained and rinsed
1 tablespoon tomato purée
1 teaspoon dried mixed herbs
salt and freshly ground black pepper

1. Put the onion and carrot in a pan, with 6 tablespoons of the vegetable stock.
2. Bring to the boil, cover and simmer for 5 minutes, or until the vegetables are tender.
3. Add the remainder of the stock and bring to the boil again. Add the pasta and turn down to a simmer.
4. Add the beans, tomato purée and herbs and simmer for 15 minutes.
5. Season to taste with salt and pepper before serving.

Cook's note:
Most canned beans come in 400 g sizes, so drain and use half in the soup and use the other half in a salad or add to a dish like Winter Vegetable Medley (page 20).

Variations:
The darker coloured beans, such as aduki, are a good contrast to the colour of the pasta. Even baked beans can be used, but do not drain them.

Points per serving: 1 1/2
Total Points per recipe: 6

Vegetable Dishes and Salads

Vegetable dishes and salads are ideal for Weight Watchers Members and only need a little imagination to lift them from the realms of the ordinary into really tasty, fresh and exciting healthy recipes.

In these recipes above all, taking the time to check what is currently in season can significantly cut the cost. If you are fortunate enough to be able to grow your own vegetables, you can save even more. Street markets are also a cheap source of fruit and vegetables and it is worth 'cultivating' your favourite trader, whose produce is always of a reliable quality, for his or her knowledge of what is at its best quality and value, as well as for occasional favours, such as very cheap or free produce that is past its best but worth having to use immediately.

Salads do not have to be restricted to the summer months. Many of the winter vegetables, with their crunchy textures, are ideal when the weather is cold. For example, grated carrot with a simple yogurt-based salad dressing, sprinkled with chopped chives or spring onions is delicious.

Most of these recipes can be eaten on their own as snacks but they can also accompany one of the main dishes, for a more substantial meal.

Winter Vegetable Medley

Serves: 4

Preparation time: 10–15 minutes + 30 minutes cooking
Calories per serving: 75

Freezing: recommended

Ⓥ

This is such a flexible recipe and its character will change according to the ingredients. The only basics are an onion and a small can of tomatoes and then you can be as creative as you like. As the finished dish is quite a bright orange colour, it looks pretty served with a green leafy vegetable.

1 onion, chopped
200 g (7 oz) canned tomatoes, chopped
1 teaspoon dried mixed herbs
300 g (10½ oz) swede
1 parsnip, cut into bite-sized chunks
1 turnip, cut into bite-sized chunks
2 carrots, cut into bite-sized chunks
½ celeriac, cut into bite-sized chunks
salt and freshly ground black pepper

1. Put the onion, tomatoes and herbs in a large pan and heat gently for 5 minutes.
2. Add the remaining vegetables to the pan, stir to mix the ingredients together and cover with a lid.
3. Simmer until all the vegetables are tender and then season to taste.

Cook's note:
This would make the basis of a good soup; cut the vegetables into smaller pieces and add more stock.

Variations:
Other vegetables that could be added or used to replace the ones in the ingredients list are celery, leek, sweet potato, squash or potato; add extra Points if using potatoes.

A tablespoon of pearl barley could be added, to give the dish more substance; add an extra ½ Point to the total.

Points per serving: 1
Total Points per recipe: 3½

Mashed Swede with Orange

Serves: 2

Preparation time: 5 minutes
+ 20 minutes cooking
Calories per serving: 50

Freezing: recommended

(v)

350 g (12 oz) swede, peeled
grated zest and juice of 1 orange
salt and freshly ground black
pepper

Swede is an under-rated
winter vegetable. It is cheap,
has a lovely warm colour
when cooked and mixes
well with other flavours.
In Scotland, this would be
called 'bashed neeps' and is
traditionally served with
haggis.

1. Cook the swede in boiling, lightly salted water for 20 minutes.
This can also be done in the microwave.
2. Drain, leaving about 2 tablespoons of water in the bottom of
the pan.
3. Mash until smooth and then add the zest and juice of the orange.
Season to taste with salt and pepper.
4. Reheat gently and serve.

Variations:
Carrots can be used instead of swede.
   Chopped fresh herbs, such as chives or parsley, can be added for
extra flavour and colour.

Points per serving: 0
Total Points per recipe: ¹/₂

Leek Salad Mimosa

Serves: 2

Preparation and cooking time:
10 minutes
Calories per serving: 85

Freezing: not recommended

(v)

2 leeks, cleaned
1 small onion, chopped
1 egg, hard-boiled
1 tablespoon Weight Watchers
   from Heinz Low-fat Salad
   Dressing or low-fat plain
   yogurt
salt and freshly ground black
   pepper

The sieved, hard-boiled egg
yolk makes a pretty garnish,
reminiscent of mimosa
blossom, hence the name.

1. Cut the leeks in thick slices and cook, with the onion, in boiling
water for 5 minutes. This can also be done in a microwave. Drain.
2. Shell the egg and cut it in half. Separate the yolk from the white.
3. Chop the egg white and add to the leeks and onion.
4. Transfer to a serving bowl and stir in the dressing or yogurt.
Season to taste with salt and pepper.
5. Put the yolk in a sieve or strainer and rub it through over the
salad.

Cook's note:
If you don't have a sieve or strainer, just chop the egg yolk as finely
as you can and sprinkle it over the salad.

Variation:
Sliced tomatoes or grated carrot could be added to the leeks and
onions, along with the egg white. You may need a little extra
dressing if you add more vegetables.

Points per serving: 1
Total Points per recipe: 2

Peruvian Potatoes

Serves: 4

Preparation time: 5 minutes
+ 25 minutes cooking
Calories per serving: 105

Freezing: recommended

Ⓥ

This colourful and spicy dish
echoes the vibrant colours
found in this South-American
country. The chilli flavour can
be adjusted to your personal
taste.

1 onion, red if possible, sliced
thinly
1 red chilli, de-seeded and sliced
finely or a few drops of
Tabasco sauce
150 ml (¼ pint) skimmed milk
1 teaspoon ground tumeric
450 g (1 lb) potatoes, red-
skinned, if possible
salt and freshly ground black
pepper

1. Put the onion, chilli or Tabasco sauce, milk and turmeric in a
saucepan. Bring to the boil, cover and simmer for 5 minutes.
2. Scrub the potatoes (but do not peel them), and cut them into
bite-size chunks.
3. Add the potatoes to the pan and continue to simmer, covered,
for 15–20 minutes, until the potatoes are tender. If the liquid level
looks low, add a little boiling water, but the finished 'sauce' should
be quite thick.
4. Taste and adjust the seasoning.

Variation:
Sweet potatoes, with their naturally red skins and bright yellow flesh,
are ideal for this dish. Use them in the winter, when they are in
season and therefore less expensive.

Points per serving: 1½
Total Points per recipe: 5½

Onion Slaw with Tofu 'Mayonnaise'

Serves: 4

Preparation time: 15 minutes
Calories per serving: 40

Freezing: not recommended

Ⓥ

The 'mayonnaise' makes a
very acceptable alternative to
the real thing and contains
fewer Calories than even a
low-calorie version.

For the 'mayonnaise':
85 g (3 oz) natural tofu (about
¼ packet)
1 tablespoon low-fat plain yogurt
1 tablespoon malt or white-wine
vinegar
1 teaspoon French or grainy
mustard
1 garlic clove or 1 teaspoon
garlic purée
salt and freshly ground black
pepper
For the salad:
175 g (6 oz) white cabbage
(about ½ small one)
½ onion, sliced thinly
1 tablespoon chopped fresh
parsley or snipped fresh
chives

1. Either put all the 'mayonnaise' ingredients in a blender or
liquidiser and blend until smooth, or mix together in a bowl.
In the latter case, you will need to use garlic purée or crush the
garlic clove.
2. For the salad, remove the thick stem from the cabbage and
slice thinly.
3. Add this, with the onion and chopped herbs, to the 'mayonnaise';
toss until evenly coated.

Variations:
Make a standard coleslaw with the cabbage, as above, adding a grated
carrot instead of the onion.
    Flavour the 'mayonnaise' with curry paste or powder and use as
a dip, for raw vegetables.
    Use the 'mayonnaise' for a potato salad.

Points per serving: ½
Total Points per recipe: 1

Chick-pea Dip with Raw Vegetables

Serves: 4

Preparation time: 15 minutes
Calories per serving: if using pitta bread (one per person) 240; if not 90

Freezing: recommended for the dip only

ⓥ

This is a variation on the well-known Greek dip hummous, but without the oiliness and, therefore, without the extra Calories.

425 g (15 oz) canned chick-peas
2 garlic cloves, or 1 small onion, chopped finely, crushed or grated
2 tablespoons Weight Watchers from Heinz Low-fat Salad Dressing (the mustard one is excellent) or mayonnaise
salt and freshly ground black pepper
fresh vegetables, e.g., carrots, celery, peppers or 4 medium pitta breads, to serve

1. Either liquidise or mash the chick-peas and their juice. If liquidising, put the onion or garlic in at the same time. If mashing, crush the garlic and chop finely or grate the onion.
2. Stir in the salad dressing or mayonnaise.
3. Season to taste with salt and pepper and put in one large bowl or individual bowls.
4. Cut the vegetables into sticks about 6 cm (2¹/₂ inches) long for dipping. If using bread, cut into bite-size pieces, which can be toasted.
5. Serve on a separate plate.

Cook's note:
If there is any dip left over, use it as a sandwich spread or mix it into stuffed baked potatoes.

Points per serving: if using pitta bread 4¹/₂; if not 2
Total Points per recipe: if using pitta bread 10; if not 7¹/₂

Celeriac and Herb Salad

Serves: 4

Preparation time: 10 minutes
Calories per serving: 15

Freezing: not recommended

ⓥ

Celeriac must be one of the ugliest vegetables around but the flavour is wonderful – an intense version of the taste of celery with a nutty, crunchy texture.

250 g (9 oz) celeriac, peeled
1 tablespoon malt vinegar
2 tablespoons chopped fresh herbs
2 tablespoons low-fat plain yogurt
salt and freshly ground black pepper

1. Grate the celeriac coarsely into a basin of water with the vinegar added (this will prevent it from going brown.)
2. Drain thoroughly when ready to make up the salad.
3. Stir in the chopped herbs, reserving a few to sprinkle on top.
4. Add the yogurt and coat all the celeriac in it.
5. Season with salt and pepper to taste and sprinkle with the reserved herbs before serving.

Cook's notes:
If you have some French mustard, stir in a teaspoonful with the yogurt.
    This makes a good starter or snack, served either with some bread or with a little cold meat.

Variation:
Weight Watchers from Heinz Salad Dressing could be used to replace the yogurt.

Points per serving: ¹/₂
Total Points per recipe: 2

Raita Salad

Serves: 4

Preparation time: 10 minutes
Calories per serving: 30

Freezing: not recommended

Ⓥ

If you go to Indian restaurants, you will be familiar with raita, the cooling side dish based on yogurt which accompanies hot spicy dishes. Serve it with some Indian bread for a delicious snack or spoon it on to lettuce leaves. Simplicity itself.

150 ml (¼ pint) low-fat plain yogurt
¼ cucumber, peeled and thinly sliced
4 small tomatoes, peeled, de-seeded and chopped
1 tablespoon chopped fresh mint
salt and freshly ground black pepper

1. Put the yogurt in a serving bowl.
2. Add the cucumber, chopped tomatoes and mint.
3. Season to taste with salt and pepper.

Cook's notes:
The easiest way to skin tomatoes is to pour boiling water over them and, after a minute, drain – the skin will peel off easily.

Make this salad just before serving as it goes 'watery' very quickly.

Points per serving: ½
Total Points per recipe: 1½

Chicory, Carrot and Sunflower Seed Salad

Serves: 2

Preparation time: 10 minutes
Calories per serving: 90; with yogurt 80

Freezing: not recommended (but the salads can be made earlier and kept in the fridge, covered with foil or film, for about 3 hours)

Ⓥ

1 small head of chicory
2 carrots
2 tablespoons Weight Watchers from Heinz Salad Dressing or 1 tablespoon orange juice and 1 tablespoon low-fat plain yogurt
1 tablespoon sunflower seeds
salt and freshly ground black pepper

This is colourful and can be made all the year round. It is surprising how much grated carrot you get from one carrot.

1. Arrange the salad on two plates – first separating the chicory leaves and arranging them like petals around the outside of the plate.
2. Grate the carrots and mix with the salad dressing or the orange juice and yogurt. Place in a pile in the middle of the 'petals'. Sprinkle the carrots with the sunflower seeds.
3. Season the salad plates with salt and pepper before serving.

Variation:
Children would have great fun in creating 'flowers'. Use watercress or shredded cabbage for the outside of the plate and grated celeriac for the centre. Or just see what you have in the fridge and create your own arranged salad.

Points per serving: 1
Total Points per recipe: 1½

Colcannon

Serves: 4

Preparation time: 10 minutes
+ 25 minutes cooking
Calories per serving: 105

Freezing: recommended

Ⓥ

This is the low-calorie version
of the traditional Irish dish.

1 onion, chopped
450 g (1 lb) potatoes, peeled
 thinly and cut into chunks
225 g (8 oz) green cabbage,
 stalk removed, leaves
 shredded
salt and freshly ground black
 pepper

1. Put the onion in a pan, with the potatoes. Cover with water, bring to the boil and boil gently for 20 minutes, or until the potatoes are soft.
2. At the same time, cook the cabbage in a little water for 8 minutes. (The cabbage could be cooked in a colander or steamer above the potatoes and onions.)
3. Drain the potatoes, leaving enough cooking water to mash them to a soft consistency.
4. Drain the cabbage and beat it into the potatoes. Season to taste with salt and pepper and serve.

Cook's note:
The vegetables can be cooked in a microwave oven, to save time and fuel.

Variations:
To make a more substantial dish, separately cook 2 chopped lean rashers of back bacon, with the chopped onion. Then mix with the potatoes and cabbage. You will need less salt to flavour. The total Points per recipe will be 10 and the Points per serving will be 2½.

   Other green, leafy vegetables could be used, such as kale or savoy cabbage.

Points per serving: 1½
Total Points per recipe: 5

Brussels Sprouts with Ham

Serves: 2

Preparation time: 5 minutes
+ 15 minutes cooking
Calories per serving: with
mustard 75; without mustard
70

Freezing: not recommended

225 g (8 oz) Brussels sprouts,
 trimmed
55 g (2 oz) lean ham, chopped
 small
1 teaspoon grainy mustard
 (optional)
freshly ground black pepper

If you are not keen on sprouts, this recipe will make them more palatable and it is easy to do. It is best to make it during the winter, when sprouts are in season. Try it at Christmas, too!

1. Cook the sprouts in a little boiling water for 8 minutes. They should still be firm and definitely not soggy.
2. Drain and toss with the chopped ham, and the mustard, if using.
3. Sauté over a low heat for a minute until hot right through.
4. Season with pepper only, as the ham is naturally salty.

Variation:
Leeks can be treated in the same way.

Cook's note:
Keep the vegetable water for stock or soup-making.

Points per serving: 1½
Total Points per recipe: 2½

Chicken and Potato Korma Salad

Serves: 4

Preparation time: 10 minutes
+ 25 minutes cooking + 30
minutes cooling
Calories per serving: 190

Freezing: not recommended

Korma is an Indian, yogurt-
based sauce. Yogurt often
curdles when it is heated but
this is added cold, so it is
foolproof.

2 medium boneless, skinless
  chicken thighs
2 teaspoons curry powder or
  paste, strength to your taste
low-fat cooking spray
1 onion, chopped
225 g (8 oz) small potatoes
  (new potatoes are best)
1 apple
150 ml (¼ pint) low-fat plain
  yogurt
salt and freshly ground black
  pepper
2 spring onions, trimmed and
  sliced (optional), to garnish

1. Preheat the grill. Rub the chicken thighs all over with curry powder
or paste. Spray with oil and grill for 15–20 minutes, turning often.
Leave to cool.
2. Meanwhile, cook the onion and the potatoes, unpeeled, in water
for 20 minutes.
3. When the chicken is cool enough, cut into strips.
4. Drain the potatoes and onions. Cut the potatoes into bite-size
pieces, when cool enough to handle. Put the chicken, potatoes and
onion in a bowl.
5. Cut the apple into thin slices, without peeling it. Add to the bowl.
6. Coat all the ingredients with the yogurt and season to taste with
salt and pepper. Sprinkle with chopped spring onions, if used.

Points per serving: 2½
Total Points per recipe: if using curry paste 10½; if not 9½

Orange and Onion Salad

Serves: 2

Preparation time: 15 minutes
Calories per serving: 150

Freezing: not recommended

Ⓥ

Fruit and vegetables mix well
in a savoury salad and the
flavour of the fruit is often
enhanced by seasoning, as the
oranges are here. Use mild
onions for this recipe.

2 large oranges
2 teaspoons oil
1 mild onion, e.g. red or
  Spanish
a few sprigs of watercress
  (optional)
salt and freshly ground black
  pepper

1. Grate the zest from the oranges and mix with the oil in a small
bowl.
2. Cut the skins from the oranges with a sharp knife, taking off the
pith, and cut the flesh into horizontal slices.
3. Cut the onion into horizontal slices and divide it into rings.
4. If using the watercress, arrange around the edge of two plates.
5. Arrange the orange slices on the top. Season well with salt and
plenty of black pepper.
6. Arrange the onion rings on the oranges and spoon over the
orange-flavoured oil.

Points per serving: 2
Total Points per recipe: 4

Meals without Meat

By cutting out the most expensive items in the shopping basket – meat, poultry and fish – vegetarian dishes are the ideal choice for low-cost cooking. You don't have to be a vegetarian to eat vegetarian food: many people these days are cutting down on the number of the times they eat meat, poultry or fish, perhaps keeping two or three days a week 'meat free'.

Vegetarians have no problem including enough protein in their diet – beans, tofu, eggs and vegetarian cheese are all good ingredients to use: beans and tofu, in particular, are low in fat and so are eminently suitable for Weight Watchers Members.

All the dishes in this chapter are main dishes. In some cases, a small portion will suffice as a snack, for example, Garlicky Baked Potatoes (page 34), but for other snacks you would be better off looking in the Vegetables chapter. I have also used some convenience foods, such as bread mixes which are used as a base for pizzas. These days bread mixes take the hard work and long waiting process out of the traditional methods, and as well as being economical, they give excellent results.

Garlicky Baked Potatoes

Serves: 2

Preparation time: 5 minutes + 1¼ hours cooking
Calories per serving: 140

Freezing: recommended

Ⓥ

1 large baking potato
2 garlic cloves, crushed or 1 teaspoon garlic purée
4 tablespoons skimmed milk
25 g (1 oz) half-fat grated cheese
salt and freshly ground black pepper

It's best to cook several potatoes at a time to make the most of heating up the oven.

1. Preheat the oven to Gas Mark 7/220°C/425°F.
2. Scrub the potato, if necessary, and slit the skin around the middle.
3. Bake for an hour, turning half-way through. (Alternatively, cook in the microwave, following the manufacturer's instructions).
4. Carefully split the potato in half and scoop the cooked flesh into a basin.
5. Add the garlic to the potato, with the skimmed milk.
6. Beat until smooth, season, and put back in the potato shells.
7. Top with grated cheese. Either bake in the oven for another 10 minutes or cook under a medium grill until golden brown.

Points per serving: 3
Total Points per recipe: 6½

Quick Onion and Baked Bean Pizzas

Makes 4 small snack pizzas

Preparation time: 10 minutes + 10–15 minutes cooking
Calories per serving: 140

Freezing: recommended

Ⓥ

1 onion, chopped
2 medium muffins
½ × 420 g can of Weight Watchers from Heinz Baked Beans
50 g (2 oz) half-fat mozzarella cheese, sliced

This is almost as simple as beans on toast but, with a little imagination, it becomes a pizza.

1. Heat the chopped onion gently in a small, covered pan, with 4 tablespoons of water, until soft. Drain.
2. Split the muffins and toast them on the cut side.
3. Mix together the onion and the baked beans and spoon on top of the muffin halves.
4. Put the slices of cheese on top of the beans and grill until the cheese is brown and bubbling.

Cook's note:
Use the other half of the beans in a soup, Bean and Pasta Soup (page 19), for example.

Points per pizza: 2½
Total Points per recipe: 9½

Potato and Spinach Curry

Serves: 4

Preparation time: 10 minutes
+ 20–25 minutes cooking
Calories per serving: 115

Freezing: recommended

v

If you go regularly to an
Indian restaurant or have a
take-away, you may recognise
this dish as *sag aloo*. Use a
ready-made curry powder or
paste, which is cheaper than
grinding your own spices.
Serve with Raita Salad (page
28), to cool the palate.

1 onion, chopped
1 garlic clove, crushed
1 tablespoon curry powder or
   paste, strength according to
   your taste
450 g (1 lb) potatoes, peeled
   and cut into small bite-sized
   pieces
250 g (9 oz) spinach, washed
salt

1. Put the onion, garlic, curry powder or paste and 4 tablespoons of
water in a pan or flameproof casserole and bring to the boil.
2. Simmer, covered, until the onion is soft.
3. Add the potatoes and stir well to distribute the spicy sauce.
A little more water can be added at this stage. Cover and cook
for 10 minutes.
4. Add the spinach to the pan and cover. It will soon shrink down
as it cooks.
5. Stir in the curry and add salt to taste.

Cook's note:
Ready-washed spinach leaves are available in supermarkets and
greengrocers however it is much cheaper to buy loose spinach and
wash it yourself. It may also need to be trimmed slightly.

Points per serving: 1½
Total Points per recipe: if using curry paste 6½; if not 5

Lemon Rice with Seasonal Vegetables

Serves: 4

Preparation time: 10–15
minutes + 20 minutes cooking
Calories per serving: 200

Freezing: recommended

v

This colourful rice could be
served on its own or as a side
dish with meat and fish dishes.
If there is any left over, add a
little low-calorie salad dressing
to make a rice salad.

200 g (7 oz) long-grain rice
1 teaspoon ground turmeric
200 g (7 oz) broccoli florets
1 carrot, sliced
grated zest and juice of 1 small
   lemon
salt and freshly ground black
   pepper

1. Cook the rice according to the packet instructions, adding the
turmeric to the cooking water. Drain well.
2. Meanwhile, cook the broccoli and carrot in a little water for about
5 minutes. (This could also be done in a microwave.) Drain.
3. Add the rice to the vegetables, with the lemon zest and juice and
heat through gently.
4. Season to taste with salt and pepper and serve.

Variation:
Shredded cabbage could replace the broccoli; swede or turnip could
replace the carrot.

Points per serving: 2½
Total Points per recipe: 10

Potato and Onion Cake with Mushrooms

Serves: 4

Preparation time: 15 minutes
+ 45 minutes cooking
Calories per serving: 245

Freezing: recommended

Ⓥ

If you are able to pick field mushrooms, they would be ideal for this dish. Never wash mushrooms or they will become soggy; simply wipe them with a clean, damp cloth. There is no need to peel them either.

low-fat cooking spray
225 g (8 oz) mushrooms, sliced
2 onions, chopped
1 garlic clove, crushed
2 tablespoons vegetable oil
150 ml (¼ pint) skimmed milk
750 g (1 lb 10 oz) potatoes, peeled thinly
salt and freshly ground black pepper

1. Preheat the oven to Gas Mark 6/200°C/400°F. Line a round ovenproof dish with foil or baking parchment. Spray with oil.
2. Mix the prepared mushrooms, onions and garlic together and heat, with 2 teaspoons of the oil and 1 tablespoon of the milk, for 5 minutes. This could be done in a microwave for 2 minutes on full power. Season to taste.
3. Slice the potatoes thinly but do not rinse them. The starch will help keep the 'cake' together.
4. Put a neat layer of potato in the bottom of the dish and season it with salt and pepper.
5. Then layer the mushroom mixture with the potatoes, seasoning each layer of potatoes. Finish with a potato layer.
6. Pour over the remaining milk and brush the top with the remaining oil. Cover with a piece of foil and bake for about 45 minutes, removing the foil for the last 15 minutes. The top should be brown and crispy and the potatoes soft.
7. Remove from the oven and leave to rest for 5 minutes.
8. Invert on to a plate, removing the base paper or foil. The base should be equally crisp. If not, just grill it lightly.

Points per serving: 3½
Total Points per recipe: 13½

Red Cabbage and Noodles

Serves: 2

Preparation time: 10 minutes
+ 15 minutes cooking
Calories per serving: 245

Freezing: recommended

Ⓥ

Chinese noodles are very quick and easy to cook, they only need to be soaked in boiling water. Stir-fries are equally quick.

100 g (3½ oz) Chinese egg noodles
low-fat cooking spray
1 garlic clove, chopped
1 green chilli, de-seeded and sliced thinly (optional)
1 onion, sliced into rings
200 g (7 oz) red cabbage, sliced thinly
1 tablespoon vinegar (any sort) or lemon juice
1 tablespoon soy sauce
2 spring onions, sliced, to garnish

1. Soak the noodles in boiling water, following the instructions on the pack. Drain.
2. Spray a wok with oil and add 3 tablespoons of water.
3. Add the garlic, chilli (if using) and onion and bring to the boil.
4. Keeping the heat high, add the red cabbage and the vinegar or lemon juice. (The acidity of the vinegar or lemon is essential to keep the cabbage red. Without it, the cabbage will be blue.)
5. After 3 minutes, stir in the drained noodles and heat through.
6. Sprinkle with soy sauce and serve the spring onions on top.

Variation:
A number of different vegetables can be used, according to your budget – choose from broccoli, baby sweetcorn, red peppers, green beans, Chinese or white cabbage or carrots.

Cook's notes:
The stir-fry can easily be stretched by adding more noodles and different vegetables, remembering to calculate any extra Points.

Seasoning with salt and pepper is not usually necessary, especially if chilli and soy sauce have been used, but taste the dish first and see what you think.

Points per serving: 2½
Total Points per recipe: 5

Vegetable Couscous

Serves: 4

Preparation time:
10 minutes + 30 minutes
cooking
Calories per serving: with
sultanas 270; without sultanas
255

Freezing: recommended

Ⓥ

**This is a North-African dish
that is spiced with chilli. Just
leave the hot spice out if you
don't like it.**

225 g (8 oz) couscous
1 onion, chopped
1 garlic clove, sliced or crushed
200 g (7 oz) canned tomatoes
2 carrots, sliced
1 turnip, cut into bite-size
  cubes
1 courgette, sliced
1 red chilli, de-seeded and cut
  into thin rings (optional)
2 teaspoons ground cinnamon
150 ml (¼ pint) vegetable stock
25 g (1 oz) sultanas (optional)
salt and freshly ground black
  pepper

1. Put the couscous in a basin and add enough cold water to cover
it by 2.5 cm (1 inch). Leave to stand for 2–3 minutes. Alternatively,
follow the pack instructions.
2. Drain and place in a steamer or colander lined with a clean tea
towel.
3. Put all the remaining ingredients, except the seasoning, in a pan
and bring to the boil. Turn down to a simmer.
4. Steam the couscous, covered, over the simmering vegetables, for
25 minutes.
5. Fork through the couscous and put it on a warmed plate or
plates.
6. Season the vegetables and spoon them over the top.

Variations:
Use the recipe for Winter Vegetable Medley (page 20) instead of the
one above. Use any combination of winter vegetables – pumpkin is
a good addition in the autumn.
   The traditional North-African couscous also includes meat, usually
lamb, with the vegetables.

Points per serving: 3
Total Points per recipe: 13

Broccoli, Mushroom and Sweetcorn Pizza

Makes: 4 main-meal pizzas

Preparation time: 15 minutes
+ 30 minutes rising + 15
minutes cooking
Calories per serving: with
white bread mix 640; with
wholemeal bread mix 565

Freezing: recommended

Ⓥ if using vegetarian cheese

**Bread mixes get better and
better. There is no long rising
time or double-kneading
of the dough and you only
need to add water. I used a
sunflower-seed bread mix, for
extra texture, but a simple
white or wholemeal mix
would be fine.**

500 g (1 lb 2 oz) white or
  wholemeal bread mix
1 tablespoon oil
1 head of broccoli, florets
  separated
175 g (6 oz) mushrooms, sliced
200 g (7 oz) canned sweetcorn
  kernels, drained
100 g (3½ oz) half-fat grated
  cheese
salt and freshly ground black
  pepper

1. Make up the bread dough, according to the pack instructions;
leave to rise.
2. Heat the oil in a frying-pan or wok and add all the prepared
vegetables. Stir-fry for 5 minutes. Season to taste. Leave on one
side.
3. Preheat the oven to Gas Mark 7/220°C/425°F. Cut the dough
into 4 pieces and roll each out to a circle. Put on an oiled baking
sheet or sheets or on shallow round tins.
4. Divide the vegetables between each and spread out.
5. Divide the cheese between the four and sprinkle it over the top.
6. Bake for 10–15 minutes.

Variation:
All sorts of vegetables can be used as a topping, from the standard
onion and tomato with herbs to peppers, aubergines and courgettes.
See what you have in the fridge and make up your own toppings.

Cook's note:
Use up the broccoli stalks in Broccoli Soup (page 11).

Points per serving: 8½
Total Points per recipe: 35

Quorn® Pilau

Serves: 4

Preparation time: 10 minutes
+ 25 minutes cooking
Calories per serving: 365;
with sweetcorn 360

Freezing: recommended

Ⓥ

**Quorn® will take on the
flavours of the dish into
which it is incorporated
and will also give a meaty
texture.**

1 tablespoon oil
1 onion, chopped
1 teaspoon ground cinnamon
225 g (8 oz) packaged Quorn®
   chunks
225 g (8 oz) long-grain rice,
   rinsed
2 teaspoons tomato purée
600 ml (1 pint) vegetable stock
325 g (11½ oz) canned garden
   peas
salt and freshly ground black
   pepper

1. Heat the oil in a pan and gently cook the onion and the cinnamon
for 5 minutes.
2. Add the Quorn® chunks and mix well together.
3. Drain the rinsed rice, add to the pan and mix well.
4. Add the tomato purée to the stock and also add this mixture to
the pan.
5. Bring to the boil, cover tightly and turn down to a simmer for
10 minutes, or until the stock has been absorbed.
6. Drain and rinse the peas and stir into the pilau until heated
right through. Season to taste with salt and pepper.

Variations:
Other fresh vegetables that would be suitable are cauliflower, carrots
and mushrooms. These should be cut into bite-size pieces; add at
the same time as the rice.
   Other canned vegetables that can be used are green beans and
sweetcorn; remember to add the extra Points if using sweetcorn.

Points per serving: 5½
Total Points per recipe: 21½

Spiced Cauliflower and Chick-peas

Serves: 4

Preparation time: 10 minutes
+ 15–20 minutes cooking
Calories per serving: 135

Freezing: not recommended

Ⓥ

**This dish has a crunchy
texture and could be used
as part of an Indian meal
or on its own.**

1 tablespoon oil
1 onion, sliced into rings
1 fresh red chilli, de-seeded and
   chopped finely, or a pinch
   of cayenne pepper or chilli
   powder
½ teaspoon ground turmeric
1 cauliflower, broken into
   florets
425 g (15 oz) canned chick-peas,
   drained
salt

1. Heat the oil in a wok or frying-pan. Add the onion and cook for
2 minutes.
2. Stir in the chilli or cayenne and turmeric, the cauliflower and 4
tablespoons of water. Cook for 10 minutes, without a lid, stirring
often.
3. Add the drained chick-peas and heat through for 2–3 minutes.
4. Season to taste with salt.

Variation:
Use a small shredded cabbage in place of the cauliflower and cook
for 5 minutes rather than 10.

Points per serving: 2½
Total Points per recipe: 9½

Fish Dishes

Fish is one of the best protein foods for Weight Watchers Members and there are many low-cost fish available for those on a budget.

White fish contains very little fat and can be cooked simply and quickly by steaming or grilling. Bargain fish in this category are skate, huss, rock and whiting. The small blocks of frozen white fish can be quite cheap too and can easily be made to look more attractive.

Although oily fish, by definition, contains fat, it is a 'friendly' fat, containing essential fatty acids called 'Omega 3' and it is in this category of fish that many bargains are to be found. Herrings, if they weren't so cheap, would be a delicacy; and they are just as delicious when smoked or cured, when they become kippers and bloaters. Even salmon, that one-time extravagance, is now farmed and can often be a bargain. Mackerel is another 'meaty' fish which can be bought cheaply. Look out for fresh sardines and whitebait, which can also be cheap when in season. (Sardines are in season March to September and whitebait are best from February until July.)

Canned fish has also been used in the recipes in this chapter. Tuna is versatile, available all the year round and comes in many forms in the can – chunks, steaks and flakes in oil, water or brine. Canned sardines have a good strong flavour and mash well to blend with other ingredients, as do pilchards.

Raw fish freezes well, so you may be able to buy it cheaply in quantity from a market or get it straight from the sea or river, to freeze and use when it is unavailable fresh.

Fish can be stretched with less expensive ingredients, such as potatoes, rice or pasta; and the more strongly flavoured oily fish stand up well to spicy seasonings.

Escabeche Herrings

Serves: 4

Preparation time: 10 minutes + 15 minutes cooking
Calories per serving: 190

Freezing: recommended

This is a method of cooking oily fish in Spain and Portugal which also provides a delicious, sharp sauce to serve with the fish. It can be eaten cold as well as hot.

4 small herrings, cleaned and heads removed
1 onion, chopped
1 garlic clove, sliced thinly
2 carrots, sliced thinly
150 ml (¼ pint) malt vinegar
salt and freshly ground black pepper

1. Grill the herrings for 3 minutes on each side.
2. Put the remaining ingredients, apart from the seasoning, in a small frying-pan and bring to the boil.
3. When boiling, add the fish and simmer, covered, for 10 minutes.
4. Season to taste with salt and pepper and serve.

Variations:
Fresh sardines can be used instead – serve three per person. Small mackerel are also good with this sauce. Remember to calculate the Points.

Weight Watchers note:
Serve with mashed potato or some pasta shapes, if Points permit.

Points per serving: 2½
Total Points per recipe: 10

Rosy Fish Pie

Serves: 4

Preparation time: 10 minutes
+ 30 minutes cooking
Calories per serving: 210

Freezing: recommended

Use an inexpensive fish, like
huss or rock, or buy those
small frozen blocks and
defrost. If you don't want to
make mashed potato from
scratch, use an instant mash
made with skimmed milk,
remembering to work out the
Points. Serve peas or green
beans as an accompaniment.

500 g (1 lb 2 oz) potatoes, peeled
1/2 swede or 3 carrots, cut into
   even-size chunks
250 g (9 oz) white fish
300 ml (1/2 pint) skimmed milk
1 tablespoon cornflour
400 g (14 oz) canned tomatoes
salt and freshly ground black
   pepper

1. Boil the potatoes in a pan, with the carrots or swede, for about
20 minutes.
2. Meanwhile, poach the fish in about 4 or 5 tablespoons of the
milk, in a covered pan, for 7–8 minutes.
3. Drain the fish, reserving the liquor, and put it in the bottom of an
ovenproof dish. Flake it and remove any skin and obvious bones.
4. Blend the cooled liquor with the cornflour in a pan and add the
canned tomatoes, cutting them up if they are not already chopped.
Bring to the boil, stirring all the time until thickened.
5. Season well, to taste, with salt and pepper and pour over the
fish.
6. Drain the potatoes, swedes or carrots – the liquid could be
used as a vegetable stock for a soup – and mash well with as much
of the remaining milk as necessary to make a soft consistency.
Season well.
7. Spoon the golden mash over the pie and make a pattern on top,
using a fork.
8. Put under a medium grill until golden brown and crisp on the top.

Variation:
Smoked fish also gives a distinctive flavour to this dish.

Cook's note:
This dish can be made half a day in advance and then heated in the
oven at Gas Mark 5/190°C/375°F for 20–25 minutes.

Points per serving: 3
Total Points per recipe: 11

Sardine Muffins

Serves: 2 as a main meal or 4 as a snack

Preparation time: 5 minutes +
10 minutes cooking
Calories per muffin: 300

Freezing: not recommended

This is a variation on sardines
on toast. It looks like a mini
pizza.

2 medium English muffins
low-fat cooking spray
1/2 onion, sliced thinly
125 g (41/2 oz) canned sardines
   in tomato sauce

1. Split the muffins in half and lightly toast the cut sides, enough
to dry the surface but not brown the muffin. Spray with oil.
2. Arrange the sliced onion over the top, return to the grill and grill
slowly until the toast is golden brown.
3. Put one sardine on each muffin (there are usually 4 sardines to a
can) or divide the sardines between the muffins.
4. Grill again, to heat the sardines.
5. Serve two half-muffins for a main course or one for a snack.

Variation:
Use pilchards in tomato sauce instead of sardines. The Points will
be the same.

Points per whole muffin: 4
Total Points per recipe: 8

Sardine Pâté

Serves: 4

Preparation time: 10 minutes
Calories per serving: with
fromage frais 85; with quark 95

Freezing: recommended

Served with oatcakes or with
crisp wholemeal toast, this
is a wonderful snack. It also
looks attractive served in
half-lemon or half-tomato
shells. Quark is a low-fat
cheese which adds creaminess
without adding too many
Points.

125 g (4½ oz) canned sardines
in tomato sauce
1 tablespoon chopped fresh
parsley
150 ml (¼ pint) low-fat plain
fromage frais or quark
2 teaspoons vinegar or lemon
juice
salt and freshly ground black
pepper

1. Empty the sardines into a basin and mash until smooth.
2. Add the parsley, fromage frais or quark and vinegar or lemon
juice, until well mixed.
3. Season to taste with salt and pepper and serve.

Points per serving: 1½
Total Points per recipe: if using fromage frais 5½; if using
quark 4

Japanese Mackerel

Serves: 4

Preparation time: 10 minutes
+ 10 minutes cooking
Calories per serving: 335

Freezing: recommended,
particularly before cooking
the mackerel

The bold flavour of mackerel,
an under-rated fish, can
easily take this spicy coating.
A fishmonger will do the
filleting for you.

2.5 cm (1-inch) piece of fresh
root ginger, peeled and grated
or chopped finely
grated zest and squeezed juice
of 1 lemon or, preferably, 1
lime
4 tablespoons soy sauce
4 tablespoons vinegar (any sort)
4 × 150 g (5 oz) medium
mackerel fillets

1. Put the ginger in a small pan. Add the zest of the lemon or lime
and the squeezed juice. Also add the soy sauce, the vinegar and
3 tablespoons of water.
2. Bring to the boil and remove from the heat. Leave to cool a little.
3. Heat the grill to medium.
4. Brush the mackerel fillets with the spicy liquid and grill for
3 minutes on each side, brushing with more liquid as they are
grilling.

Weight Watchers note:
If Points permit, serve this with some plain boiled rice. If not, a
salad would make a good accompaniment – perhaps Raita Salad
(page 28).

Variations:
Any oily fish could be used – herrings (3 Points per medium fillet)
or even salmon steaks or fillets (3½ Points per medium steak or
fillet).
 This dish can be cooked on the barbecue in warmer weather.

Points per serving: 6
Total Points per recipe: 24

Cod Chowder

Serves: 4

Preparation time: 10 minutes
+ 25 minutes cooking
Calories per serving: 110

Freezing: not recommended

A chowder is, strictly, a soup but it is quite substantial, so I feel justified in including it as a main dish. A fishmonger will skin the fish for you.

2 streaky bacon rashers, de-
    rinded and chopped
1 onion, chopped
425 ml (^{3}/$_4$ pint) skimmed milk
225 g (8 oz) cod fillet, or other
    white fish, skinned and cut
    into chunks
1 large potato, peeled and cut
    into small cubes
2 bay leaves (optional)
1 tablespoon chopped fresh
    parsley (optional)
freshly ground black pepper

1. Put the chopped bacon in a pan and heat gently, until the fat starts to run.
2. Add the chopped onion and cook gently for 5 minutes, or until the onion is soft but not brown.
3. Add the milk and 150 ml (^{1}/$_4$ pint) water and bring to the boil. Turn down to a simmer.
4. Add the fish and the potato and the bay leaves, if used.
5. Simmer for 20 minutes, covered, by which time the fish should be cooked and the potatoes soft.
6. Add the parsley, if used. This is not absolutely necessary but it does add colour to what is otherwise a rather white-looking soup.
7. Season to taste – probably only pepper will be required. Remove the bay leaves before serving.

Variations:
Smoked fish can be used, giving 4 Points per serving, and, when you're not economising, prawns make a good alternative (4^1/$_2$ Points per serving).

Points per serving: 4
Total Points per recipe: 16^1/$_2$

Kipper Kedgeree

Serves: 4

Preparation time: 10 minutes
+ 20–25 minutes cooking
Calories per serving: 400

**Freezing: recommended,
without the hard-boiled egg**

This rice dish is usually made with smoked haddock but kipper fillets work very well too.

225 g (8 oz) long-grain rice
2 teaspoons oil
1 onion, chopped
2 x 120 g (4 oz) kipper fillets
150 ml (^{1}/$_4$ pint) low-fat plain
    fromage frais
1 tablespoon chopped fresh
    parsley
1 egg, hard-boiled
freshly ground black pepper

1. Rinse the rice and leave to drain.
2. Heat the oil in a pan and put in the onion. Cook gently for 5 minutes, until cooked but not browned.
3. Stir in the drained rice and stir to mix in.
4. Add 300 ml (^{1}/$_2$ pint) water and bring to the boil. Cover and simmer for about 20 minutes, adding the kipper fillets after 15 minutes. Check occasionally in case a little more boiling water needs to be added as it is cooking but after 20 minutes all the water should have been absorbed.
5. Take the fillets from the pan and carefully remove the skin. Put them back in the pan and fork through to break up the kipper into flakes.
6. Stir in the fromage frais and parsley and heat through gently. Season to taste.
7. Shell the egg and halve. Take out the yolk and chop the white.
8. Add the white to the rice. Put the kedgeree on a serving plate or plates and either sieve the yolk over the top or chop it finely and sprinkle it over.

Points per serving: 6
Total Points per recipe: 23^1/$_2$

Tuna and Bean Bake

Serves: 2

Preparation time: 5 minutes
+ 20 minutes cooking
Calories per serving: 225

Freezing: recommended

**Canned tuna with white
beans and raw onion is often
served as a salad starter in
Italy. This is a hot version,
with a crunchy topping. The
onion is also meant to be on
the crunchy side. Serve with
a fresh salad.**

100 g (3½ oz) canned tuna in
   brine, drained
1 onion, chopped
420 g can of Weight Watchers
   from Heinz Baked Beans
2 tablespoons fresh white
   breadcrumbs
25 g (1 oz) half-fat cheese,
   grated

1. Preheat the oven to Gas Mark 6/200°C/400°F.
2. Mix together the tuna and the onion and put in the bottom of a
baking dish.
3. Spoon over the baked beans.
4. Mix the breadcrumbs and cheese together and spoon evenly over
the top.
5. Bake for 20 minutes, or until the top is golden brown.

Cook's note:
To make breadcrumbs, use slices of stale brown or white bread and
either whizz them round in a food processor or grate them.
Breadcrumbs can be bought but it is cheaper to make them
yourself. They can be kept in a plastic bag
in the freezer, so you can take out a handful at a time when you
need them.

Points per serving: 3
Total Points per recipe: 6

Herring Roe Omelette

Serves: 1

Preparation time: 5 minutes
+ 10 minutes cooking
Calories per serving: 275; with
canned roes 305

Freezing: not recommended

**Serve with a fresh wholemeal
bread roll (don't forget to add
the Points).**

100 g (3½ oz) soft herring roes
   or 125 g (4½ oz) canned
   herring roes, drained
1 teaspoon plain flour
low-fat cooking spray
1 teaspoon Worcestershire sauce
2 eggs
salt and freshly ground black
   pepper

1. Rinse the roes and pick out any threads. Pat dry and coat in flour.
2. Spray a frying-pan with oil and, when hot, toss in the roes.
3. Cook for 2–3 minutes and then put on one side and spoon over
the Worcestershire sauce. Keep warm.
4. Beat the eggs with 2 tablespoons of water and season with salt
and pepper.
5. Spray the pan again with oil and, when hot, pour in the eggs.
6. Draw the cooked edges into the middle and, when soft but set,
put the roes in the middle.
7. Fold in half and serve on a warm plate.

Variations:
Many types of fish can be used as omelette fillings, but smoked
fish, like haddock or cod, have a particular affinity with eggs.
These can be cooked quickly in a microwave before being added
to the omelette.
   The same fish as above can be mixed into scrambled egg.

Weight Watchers note:
A heavy, non-stick pan is a good investment for this kind of recipe
as far less oil is needed to cook food without burning or sticking.

Points per serving: 4½
Total Points per recipe: 4½

Quick Mackerel Snack

Serves: 2

Preparation time: 10 minutes
Calories per serving: 545

Freezing: not recommended

A quick, refreshing and nourishing lunch for a hot or busy day when you don't feel like cooking.

2 × 150 g (5 oz) fillets, hot-smoked mackerel (the type that does not need cooking)
1 red-skinned eating apple
1 teaspoon vinegar (any sort) or lemon juice
1 celery stick (optional)
1 tablespoon Weight Watchers from Heinz Salad Cream
2 crisp, bowl-shaped lettuce leaves or 4 tablespoons shredded lettuce
salt and freshly ground black pepper

1. Remove and discard the skin from the mackerel. Cut into strips and put in a bowl.
2. Quarter and core the apple and cut into thin slices or chunks. Toss in the vinegar or lemon juice, to prevent it from browning, and add to the bowl.
3. Slice the celery thinly, if used, and add to the bowl.
4. Coat all the ingredients in the bowl with the salad cream.
5. Season to taste with salt and pepper.
6. Put a lettuce leaf on each plate or arrange the shredded lettuce with a well in the middle. Spoon in the fish filling and serve immediately.

Variations:
Use kipper fillets or any canned fish for this dish.
   Weight Watchers from Heinz Mayonnaise or Salad Dressing can be substituted for the salad cream.

Points per serving: 6¹/₂
Total Points per recipe: 13

Spiced Grilled Fish

Serves: 2

Preparation time: 5 minutes + 10 minutes marinating + 10 minutes cooking
Calories per serving: 135

Freezing: not recommended

This simple mix rubbed into fish fillets before grilling seems to go well with white as well as oily fish.

2 × 120 g (4 oz) fish fillets, e.g. herring, whiting or cod
1 teaspoon ground cinnamon
1 orange
1 tablespoon chopped fresh mint or 2 teaspoons mint sauce concentrate
salt and freshly ground black pepper

1. Rinse the fillets and pat dry.
2. Mix together the cinnamon, grated zest of the orange and the mint.
3. Rub into both sides of each fillet and leave for 10 minutes.
4. Squeeze the juice from the orange and drizzle a little over each fillet before grilling.
5. Heat the grill to medium and cook the fillets for 3 minutes on one side.
6. Turn and sprinkle with more juice and grill for a further 3 minutes.
7. Season lightly with salt and pepper and serve with any remaining juice poured over.

Points per serving: with herring or cod 1¹/₂; with whiting 1
Total Points per recipe: with herring or cod 3¹/₂; with whiting 2

Meat and Poultry Dishes

If you look at an itemised supermarket till-receipt, the meat and poultry items are almost always the most expensive. Doubly difficult for a Weight Watcher Member who is counting costs is the fact that the less expensive cuts are often the ones with the most fat.

The best solution is to use just a little meat or poultry and fill the dish out with less expensive ingredients, such as seasonal vegetables and/or starchy foods, such as potatoes, pasta, pulses and rice.

A lot of mince is now quite low in fat and, whether it is beef, lamb, pork, chicken or turkey, it can easily be stretched by adding more vegetables, as in Lamb Beetburgers (page 59). Many people are now eating less meat and it is a good idea to restrict the number of meat dishes to about five a week at the most. This will cut down on the housekeeping bills and also be better for your health.

As regards cuts of meat and poultry, choose those with the least amount of fat. With red meats, some cuts require long, slow cooking to tenderise them. Under certain circumstances, it might be better to choose canned meat, like casserole steak, therefore saving on the fuel bills. All canned food now carries a nutrition label and so it is easy to see how many Calories are contained in each can or each 100 g (3½ oz).

Poultry is often sold skinless and this is ideal for people on a diet. Where I have used poultry in this selection of recipes, I have used little in comparison with the other ingredients.

Offal, in particular liver and kidneys, is a good source of low-fat meat. I realise that for many people it is a 'turn off' but if you do like it, simply grill with accompanying vegetables or salad or thread on skewers with a selection of vegetables and serve as kebabs, with a side serving of plain boiled rice. I have included one recipe for a stir-fry (Lamb's Liver Stir-fry, page 63) but other meat could be substituted for the liver.

Chicken and Potato Casserole

Serves: 4

Preparation time: 10 minutes + 1 hour cooking
Calories per serving: 230

Freezing: recommended

Although this dish takes longer to cook than most of the recipes, it requires very little attention once it is in the oven. It is a comforting winter dish. Serve with a green vegetable, such as Brussels sprouts, cabbage or leeks.

600 g (1 lb 5 oz) potatoes, peeled thinly and cut into chunks
low-fat cooking spray
4 skinless, boneless chicken thighs, weighing about 350 g (12 oz) in total
4 whole garlic cloves
2 onions, quartered
2 tablespoons chopped fresh herbs, e.g., parsley, mint, rosemary, thyme and/or chives
150 ml (¼ pint) skimmed milk
salt and freshly ground black pepper

1. Preheat the oven to Gas Mark 4/180°C/350°F. Cook the potatoes in boiling water for 5 minutes. Drain, reserving 150 ml (¼ pint) of the liquor.
2. Spray an ovenproof dish with oil and arrange the potatoes and potato liquor, the chicken, garlic and onions in it.
3. Mix together the chopped herbs and milk and pour over. Season with salt and pepper to taste. Cover with a butter paper and bake for 45 minutes, taking off the paper for the last 20 minutes.

Points per serving: 4½
Total Points per recipe: 18

Greek Lemon Chicken

Serves: 4

Preparation time: 20 minutes
+ 1 hour cooking + overnight cooling
Calories per serving: 145

Freezing: recommended for cooked chicken only

This refreshing cold dish is ideal to make when there is a special offer on chickens. It's surprising how far one will stretch.

1.25 kg (2 lb 12 oz) fresh or frozen and defrosted chicken
1 lemon
low-fat cooking spray
200 ml (7 fl oz) low-fat plain yogurt
1 piece of cucumber, about 5 cm (2 inches) long, cut into small cubes
1 tablespoon fresh chopped parsley or coriander
salt and freshly ground black pepper

1. Put the lemon in the body cavity of the chicken. Spray the outside with oil and season with salt and pepper.
2. Roast according to the pack instructions – usually at Gas Mark 5/190°C/375°F for 45 minutes per 1 kg (2.2 lb) plus 20 minutes.
3. Let the cooked chicken cool thoroughly, leaving the lemon inside. Then put it in the fridge overnight.
4. The next day, remove the cooked flesh from the chicken, discarding the skin, if possible, and cut into bite-size pieces. You will need about 75 g (2³/₄ oz) per person. Put the chicken carcass and lemon to one side.
5. Put the yogurt in a bowl and slice in the lemon, including the peel. Mash the two together or mix in a processor or liquidiser.
6. Stir in the cucumber cubes and the chopped herbs, reserving a teaspoonful, and season to taste.
7. Mix the chicken and the sauce together and put on a serving plate.
8. Garnish with the remaining herbs.

Cook's notes:
There may be enough cooked chicken left for sandwich fillings, a pizza topping or a pasta sauce.
   Use the carcass to make chicken stock, by cooking with water, a quartered onion and carrot and some herbs, if available. This can then be used for any of the soups in the soup section, apart from Split Pea and Ham.

Variation:
Add a teaspoon of curry paste to the sauce, to make a Weight Watchers' version of Coronation Chicken, with a total of 10 Points per recipe.

Points per serving: 2¹/₂
Total Points per recipe: 9¹/₂

Lamb Beetburgers

Serves: 4

Preparation time: 10 minutes
+ 15 minutes cooking
Calories per serving: 130

Freezing: recommended (before cooking)

The beetroot gives these burgers the most brilliant pink colour. They look a picture when served with green salad. If you can spare the Points, pop them into a wholemeal bun. The Points for a medium burger bun are 2.

225 g (8 oz) lean minced lamb
1 boiled beetroot, grated coarsely
4 heaped tablespoons fresh breadcrumbs
1 teaspoon mint sauce concentrate
salt and freshly ground black pepper

1. Mix all the ingredients together in a basin, until well blended together.
2. Divide into 4 or 8 and shape each portion into a burger shape.
3. Heat the grill to medium and cook for 5 minutes on each side (8 burgers) or 7 minutes on each side (4 burgers).

Cook's note:
Put the burgers on a piece of foil under the grill. Pour off the excess fat from the foil before serving.

Variations:
Use other types of mince with the beetroot and complement with a teaspoon of appropriate flavouring, for example, lean beef mince with a spoonful of mustard, chicken mince with a teaspoon of dried thyme or Quorn® mince with chopped chives.

Points per serving: 3
Total Points per recipe: 11

Pork Ribs with a Spice Rub

Serves: 2

Preparation time: 5 minutes
+ 30 minutes marinating
+ 15 minutes cooking
Calories per serving: 425

Freezing: recommended

This could be cooked on the barbecue in the summer. Choose ribs that have plenty of meat on them and not too much fat.

4 × 75 g (2³/₄ oz) large pork
   ribs or 8 × 60 g (2¹/₄ oz)
   small ones
1 teaspoon salt
1 teaspoon ground black pepper
1 teaspoon paprika
a pinch of chilli powder
   (optional)
1 teaspoon ground cinnamon
1 teaspoon dried mixed herbs

1. Mix together all the herbs and spices and rub well into the ribs.
2. Leave to marinate for about 30 minutes, or longer if possible.
3. Grill under a medium heat, turning frequently.

Variation:
Use the spice rub for any meat or fish to be grilled.

Weight Watchers notes:
Serve with Weight Watchers from Heinz Tomato Ketchup mixed with a teaspoon of Worcestershire sauce or half a lemon.

   One of the salads in the vegetables and salads chapter, or a simple green salad, tossed with a tablespoon of Weight Watchers from Heinz Salad Dressing, would make a suitable accompaniment.

Points per serving: 3
Total Points per recipe: 6

Golden Chicken Pasta

Serves: 4

Preparation time: 10 minutes
+ 20 minutes cooking
Calories per serving: 280

Freezing: recommended

If there is any cooked chicken left from Greek Lemon Chicken (page 59), it could be used in this recipe.

225 g (8 oz) pasta shapes or
   macaroni
1 onion, chopped
2 carrots, grated
2 teaspoons tomato purée
¹/₂ teaspoon dried mixed herbs
125 g (4¹/₂ oz) cooked chicken,
   cut into bite-size pieces
salt and freshly ground black
   pepper

1. Cook the pasta according to the pack instructions. Drain when ready, keeping warm if the sauce is not ready.
2. Meanwhile, put the onion, carrots, 4 tablespoons of water, tomato purée and herbs into another pan and cook slowly, covered, for about 10 minutes, until the vegetables are soft.
3. Add the cooked chicken and heat in the 'golden' sauce, adding a little more water if the sauce looks dry.
4. Toss together with the cooked pasta and season to taste with salt and pepper. Serve while hot.

Variation:
The 'golden' sauce could be mixed with canned tuna or with other cooked meat or even, for a vegetarian, on its own.

Points per serving: 2¹/₂
Total Points per recipe: 10

Chicken Pancakes

Serves: 2

Preparation time: 10 minutes
+ 15 minutes cooking
Calories per serving: 175

Freezing: recommended, without the vegetables

If you have eaten in a Chinese restaurant, you will be familiar with the thin, papery pancakes served with 'crispy duck'. These can now be bought separately and make good 'wrappers' for a selection of foods. Eat as a snack, in your fingers.

1 medium boneless, skinless chicken thigh
low-fat cooking spray
$1/2$ teaspoon soy sauce
$1/4$ teaspoon ground ginger
4 Chinese pancakes
$1/4$ white cabbage, very thinly sliced or shredded
1 carrot, grated
25 g (1 oz) bean sprouts
1 tablespoon hoisin sauce or brown sauce or tomato ketchup
salt and freshly ground black pepper

1. Spray the chicken with the cooking spray.
2. Mix together the soy sauce and ginger and brush or rub this over the chicken.
3. Grill for about 15 minutes under a medium heat, turning occasionally, until the chicken is cooked through. Check by piercing with a skewer: the juices should be clear and the flesh should have no trace of pink.
4. Lay out the four pancakes.
5. Mix the vegetables together.
6. Spread each pancake thinly with the sauce and divide the vegetables into four. Put on top of the sauce.
7. Cut the cooked chicken into thin strips and put on top of the vegetables.
8. Season with salt and pepper and roll up.

Variations:
Use other salad vegetables as a filling.
   Lamb's Liver Stir-fry (opposite) would make a different filling for the Chinese Pancakes.

Weight Watchers note:
The remaining pancakes freeze well and can be used for a variety of fillings.

Points per serving: 2$1/2$
Total Points per recipe: 4$1/2$

Lamb's Liver Stir-fry

Serves: 2

Preparation time: 10 minutes
+ 10–15 minutes cooking
Calories per serving: 205

Freezing: not recommended

In this dish, a very little meat is stretched with plenty of vegetables. Because it takes so little time to cook, nearly all the vegetables' nutrients are retained. If you have Points to spare, Chinese noodles can be added to the stir-fry. These just need to be soaked in boiling water and then drained.

low-fat cooking spray
1 onion, sliced thinly
1 teaspoon ground ginger
125 g (4$1/2$ oz) lamb's liver, cut into strips
2 carrots, sliced thinly
$1/2$ cauliflower, broken into florets
2 leeks, sliced thinly
250 g (9 oz) spring greens or any green, leaf vegetable
1 tablespoon soy sauce
2 spring onions, to garnish (optional)

1. Spray a non-stick frying-pan or wok with cooking spray. Heat and add the onion, ginger and 3 tablespoons of water. Cook for 3 minutes.
2. Add the liver and cook for a further 2 minutes over a high heat.
3. Add the prepared vegetables one at a time – carrots first, followed by cauliflower, then leeks and finally the greens – allowing the pan to get hot again between each addition.
4. Finally, add the soy sauce.
5. Sprinkle the spring onions over each serving, if using.

Variation:
Pig's liver or chicken livers make a good alternative to lamb's liver.

Points per serving: 2$1/2$
Total Points per recipe: 5

Chicken Pizzaiola

Serves: 2

Preparation time: 10 minutes
+ 15 minutes cooking
Calories per serving: 345;
with olives 350

Freezing: recommended

This has a distinctive Italian
flavour. It uses very little meat
and most of the flavour comes
from the vegetables. If you
have enough Points in hand,
sprinkle each bowl with a
teaspoon of grated half-fat
cheese which is 1/2 Point per
serving.

low-fat cooking spray
125 g (4½ oz) chicken strips
1 green pepper, de-seeded and
  cut into strips
1 garlic clove, chopped
100 g (3½ oz) mushrooms
200 g (7 oz) canned tomatoes
1 teaspoon dried mixed herbs
6 pitted olives (optional)
salt and freshly ground black
  pepper
125 g (4½ oz) pasta, spaghetti,
  noodles or shapes, to serve

1. Spray a frying-pan with the cooking spray and heat.
2. Add the chicken and pepper strips. Cook for 4 minutes, until
lightly browned.
3. Add the garlic and the mushrooms and cook for a further
2 minutes, using a little more spray, if necessary.
4. Chop the tomatoes slightly and add to the pan, with their juice,
the herbs and the olives, if using.
5. Simmer for 5 minutes and then season to taste with salt and
pepper.
6. While the sauce is cooking, cook the pasta in another pan,
following the pack instructions.
7. Drain the pasta and divide it between two bowls.
8. Spoon the pizzaiola sauce over the pasta.

Variation:
Turkey stir-fry strips can be cooked in the same way.

Points per serving: 3½
Total Points per recipe: 7

Tyrolean Dumplings

Serves: 4

Preparation time: 10 minutes
+ 20–25 minutes cooking
Calories per serving: 170

**Freezing: recommended for
uncooked dumplings**

A really well-flavoured stock
is needed for these dumplings.
I suggest you use a ham hock
cooked with a carrot, onion
and bay leaf. Take off the meat
and use it in the dumplings
and strain the stock to use as
the cooking medium.

1 egg
150 ml (¼ pint) skimmed milk
175 g (6 oz) stale bread, grated
  or processed into crumbs
100 g (3½ oz) cooked ham or
  bacon
1 tablespoon chopped fresh
  parsley
100–115 g (3½–4 oz) plain
  flour
850 ml (1½ pints) well-
  flavoured stock
freshly ground black pepper

1. Beat the egg with the milk in a bowl and add the breadcrumbs.
2. Leave for a minute and then add the bacon or ham and the
parsley.
3. Gradually add the flour, to make a soft consistency.
4. Season mainly with pepper as the bacon or ham will be salty.
5. With wet hands, shape the dumplings into balls about the size
of a walnut.
6. Bring the stock to the boil in a large pan and, when almost
boiling, flour the outside of the dumplings.
7. Lower the dumplings gently into the stock and simmer for about
20 minutes.
8. Eat like soup, from a bowl with a spoon.

Variation:
Use mushrooms or chopped spinach in place of the bacon. For
vegetarian dumplings, cook in a good vegetable stock. Points per
serving will be 2.

Points per serving: 3
Total Points per recipe: 11

Turkey Pittas

Serves: 4

Preparation time: 10 minutes
+ 10 minutes cooking
Calories per serving: 220

**Freezing: recommended
(without the salad and yogurt)**

**Pitta bread makes a good
'envelope' for all sorts of
snacks and is ideal for picnics
and packed meals. Turkey
stir-fry strips are widely
available or use cooked
turkey after Christmas.**

low-fat cooking spray
200 g (7 oz) turkey strips
1 onion, sliced thinly
4 tablespoons low-fat plain
    yogurt
1 tablespoon brown sauce
4 medium pitta breads
4 lettuce leaves, shredded
salt and freshly ground black
    pepper

1. Spray a pan with the cooking spray and heat. Cook the turkey over a high heat, until browned.
2. Put in a bowl, with the sliced onion, yogurt and brown sauce. Season to taste.
3. Cut the pittas in half and open up the 'pockets'.
4. Fill each half with the turkey mixture and garnish the top with shredded lettuce.

Variations:
Another low-cost idea for a meaty filling is crisply cooked streaky bacon with shredded salad leaves of your choice. Just remember to count the Points.

Points per serving: 3½
Total Points per recipe: 13½

Stuffed Marrow

Serves: 4

Preparation time: 10 minutes
+ 1 hour cooking
Calories per serving: 195

**Freezing: recommended, if
slightly undercooked**

**The stuffing could be used
for other vegetables, such as
peppers or courgettes.**

1 kg (2¼ lb) marrow
225 g (8 oz) minced beef or lamb
425 g (15 oz) canned Weight
    Watchers from Heinz Baked
    Beans
1 onion, chopped finely
1 teaspoon dried mixed herbs
low-fat cooking spray
salt and freshly ground black
    pepper

1. Peel the marrow, cut in half lengthways and scoop out the seeds.
2. Mix the meat, beans, onion and herbs and season with salt and pepper.
3. Put half the stuffing in each half of the marrow and put back together again.
4. Wrap in foil, sprayed with the cooking spray.
5. Put in an ovenproof dish or tin and bake at Gas Mark 4/180°C/ 350°F for one hour.
6. Cut into slices to serve.

Points per serving: 3½
Total Points per recipe: 13

Baking and Puddings

In this section, there are recipes which may seem 'sinful' but are sensibly balanced. There are so many ingredients now which have the feel of luxury but are, in fact, quite low in Calories and fat; fromage frais and quark are two such ingredients.

Fresh fruit is obviously the ideal dessert for people on a diet and at the peak of its season fruit is bound to be not only of the highest quality and nutritional value, but also cheap. Just arranging prepared fruit imaginatively on a plate can lift it from the mundane to the luxurious.

Cakes do not have to be rich in fat. There are two delicious loaves here which are so good that they do not need to be spread with butter (see Malt Loaf, page 76 and Banana Bread, page 76) and the Spice Scones (page 79) would make a good base for fresh fruit or low-sugar jams.

So, although the recipes in this chapter may seem as though they should be out of bounds, they can all be eaten without spoiling your diet!

Pear Fans

Serves: 1

Preparation time: 10 minutes
Calories per serving: 115

Freezing: not recommended

Ⓥ if using vegetarian quark

1 ripe pear
1 teaspoon lemon juice
1 tablespoon quark (low-fat soft cheese)
1 tablespoon low-calorie raspberry jam

Cheese and pears go together very well.

1. Peel the pear and cut in half lengthways.
2. Remove the core with a teaspoon and brush all cut surfaces with lemon juice to prevent them from going brown.
3. Blend the quark and jam together and spoon into a circle on a plate.
4. Cut the pear into thin slices lengthways but keep the stalk-end uncut.
5. On the palm of your hand, spread out the 'fan' and place both 'fan' halves attractively on the raspberry cheese.

Variation:
If you can't find quark, use any other low-fat soft cheese but not cottage cheese.

Points per serving: 2$\frac{1}{2}$
Total Points per recipe: 2$\frac{1}{2}$

Lemon Fluff

Serves: 4

Preparation and cooking time:
15 minutes + 5 minutes cooking + 30 minutes chilling
Calories per serving: 105; with artificial sweetener 10

Freezing: not recommended

11.8 g sachet of gelatine
100 g (3$\frac{1}{2}$ oz) sugar or the equivalent in artificial sweetener
juice of 2 small lemons
2 egg whites

1. Put 300 ml ($\frac{1}{2}$ pint) of water in a pan and sprinkle over the gelatine.
2. Add the sugar or sweetener and the thinly peeled zest of the lemons (use a potato peeler and do not use any of the bitter white pith).
3. Heat gently, without boiling, until the sugar and the gelatine have dissolved.
4. Strain into a mixing bowl and leave to cool.
5. Add the strained lemon juice and the egg whites and whisk until thick and pale. It helps to put the bowl in another bowl containing ice cubes. Keeping the temperature down prevents it from getting too fluffy. This stage may take about 10 minutes.
6. Pour into a serving bowl or individual dishes and chill for 30 minutes.

Variation:
Other citrus fruits, such as oranges, limes or grapefruit, can be used. The sweetness will need to be adjusted for different fruits. For example, less sugar or sweetener would be needed for oranges.

Points per serving: if using sugar 1$\frac{1}{2}$; if not 0
Total Points per recipe: if using sugar 5$\frac{1}{2}$; if not 0

Rhubarb Compote

Serves: 3

Preparation time: 5 minutes
+ 10 minutes cooking
Calories per serving: 25

Freezing: recommended, if
slightly undercooked

Ⓥ

300 g (10½ oz) young, pink
rhubarb
2 tablespoons orange juice or
grated zest and squeezed
juice of 1 orange
artificial sweetener

'Compote' is just another way
of saying 'stewed' but it is
critical with rhubarb that it
is cooked slowly, otherwise
you will finish with a mush.
This can be eaten hot or cold,
served with custard or Weight
Watchers from Heinz Ice
Cream, if you have enough
Points.

1. Wipe the rhubarb and cut into 2.5 cm (1-inch) pieces.
2. Put in a saucepan, with the orange juice, or, if using an orange,
the zest and juice of the fruit.
3. Bring to the boil, cover and simmer for 5–10 minutes.
4. Sweeten to taste with artificial sweetener. This will depend on
your palate and also on the natural sweetness of the fruit and juice.

Cook's notes:
Do not add the sweetener before cooking or it will develop a bitter
taste.
    If you do overcook the rhubarb, mix it with some thick custard,
to make a rhubarb fool. Remember to add the Points for the
custard.

Variation:
Add a medium sliced banana (1½ Points) to the compote. The
flavours are complementary. Points per serving will be the same.

Points per serving: ½
Total Points per recipe: ½

Winter Fruit Salad

Serves: 4

Preparation and cooking time:
20 minutes
Calories per serving: 75

Freezing: not recommended

Ⓥ

If you have a street market
near to where you live, this is
the cheapest place to buy fresh
fruit and vegetables. However,
a supermarket is an easier
place to buy only one of
everything.

1 stick of rhubarb
1 tablespoon water or orange
juice
1 large orange
1 medium banana
juice of 1 small lemon
1 eating apple, red-skinned,
if possible
1 pear
artificial sweetener (optional)

1. Cut the rhubarb into 2.5 cm (1-inch) lengths and cook gently in
the water or orange juice for 5 minutes or until just soft. This can
be done in a microwave.
2. Transfer to a dish.
3. Peel the orange as thinly as possible and, with a sharp knife,
segment the flesh so that only the fruit and juice go into the bowl.
4. Slice the banana and toss it in lemon juice before adding it to
the bowl.
5. Quarter the apple and pear and remove the cores. Cut into thin
slices.
6. Add to the bowl, with any juices, and the remaining lemon juice.
7. Taste the juice and add sweetener, if necessary.

Weight Watchers note:
This could be served with Weight Watchers from Heinz Ice Cream
or with low-fat plain yogurt. Add the extra Points as necessary.

Points per serving: 1
Total Points per recipe: 4

Gooseberry Fool

Serves: 4

Preparation time: 10 minutes
+ 15 minutes cooking
Calories per serving: 45

Freezing: recommended

450 g (1 lb) green gooseberries
1 elderflower head (optional)
artificial sweetener, to taste
200 ml (7 fl oz) low-fat plain
  fromage frais

Make this in May or June
when gooseberries are at their
cheapest. You may be able to
'pick your own' at a fruit
farm. If you can find an elder
tree, cook a flower head with
the fruit. By good fortune,
elderflowers are in blossom at
the same time as gooseberries
are ripe and the flavours go so
well together.

1. Put the gooseberries (no need to top and tail), elderflower head
and 5 tablespoons of water into a pan. Bring to the boil and simmer
for 10 minutes, until the gooseberries are mushy.
2. Remove the flowerhead, if used, and rub the gooseberries
through a sieve into a bowl.
3. Sweeten to taste and leave to cool.
4. Stir in the fromage frais, until well blended. Spoon into serving
dishes and eat immediately.

Points per serving: 1½
Total Points per recipe: 6

Blackberry and Apple Oat Crumble

Serves: 4

Preparation time: 10 minutes
+ 30 minutes cooking
Calories per serving: 480

Freezing: recommended

(V)

Make this in the autumn,
when you can go out
blackberrying and probably
pick up some windfall apples
for nothing.

4 large apples (eating apples are
  best but use cookers if you
  wish)
175 g (6 oz) blackberries
115 g (4 oz) plain flour
1 teaspoon cinnamon
55 g (2 oz) porridge oats or
  medium oatmeal
85 g (3 oz) butter
85 g (3 oz) sugar

1. Preheat the oven to Gas Mark 5/190°C/375°F. Peel and quarter
the apples. Remove the core and cut into 1 cm (½-inch) chunks.
2. Rinse the blackberries and put them in the bottom of an
ovenproof dish. Add the apple chunks and mix together gently.
Add 4 tablespoons of water.
3. Put the flour, cinnamon and oats or oatmeal in a bowl.
4. Rub in the butter, until the mixture resembles breadcrumbs. Stir
in the sugar. (The crumble can also be made in a food processor or
in an electric food mixer.)
5. Spoon the crumble over the fruit and tidy the edges of the dish.
6. Bake for 30 minutes or until the crumble is golden brown on
top. By this time, the fruit should also be cooked but still have
some 'bite'.

Weight Watchers note:
You may like to sweeten the fruit with artificial sweetener just
before eating. Low-fat spread and granular sweetener could be used
in the crumble but the texture would not be the same. The Points
per serving would be 4½.

Variations:
Many types of fruit can be used in crumble, from rhubarb in the
spring, through soft fruit in the summer to orchard fruit in the
autumn.

Points per serving: 9½
Total Points per recipe: 38½

Apple Snow

Serves: 2

Preparation time: 5 minutes
+ 10 minutes cooking
+ 30 minutes cooling
Calories per serving: 60

Freezing: recommended for
the apple purée only

Ⓥ

1 large cooking apple
1 teaspoon ground cinnamon
  (optional)
artificial sweetener
1 egg white

This basic apple purée mixture
is very versatile. It can be
served as an apple sauce with
savoury dishes or eaten with
breakfast cereals, mixed with
custard or fromage frais as a
fool or simply eaten on its own.

1. Peel, quarter and core the apple.
2. Cut into thin slices and put them in a pan with 2 tablespoons
of water and cinnamon, if using. Bring to the boil, cover and then
turn down to a simmer for 5–10 minutes, until the apples 'fall'
or go mushy.
3. Beat well until smooth and add artificial sweetener, to taste.
Leave to cool.
4. Whisk the egg white until stiff and fold it into the apple just
before serving.

Cook's note:
To cool the cooked apple quickly, stand the pan in a sink of cold
water and, if possible, add some ice cubes to the water.

Variation:
Other purées which can be made into a 'snow' are rhubarb, plums
and damsons. Ripe strawberries can also be used and do not need
cooking.

Points per serving: 1
Total Points per recipe: 2

Double Orange Dessert

Serves: 1

Preparation time: 10 minutes
Calories per serving: 135

Freezing: not recommended

Ⓥ

1 orange
125 g (4 oz) low-fat plain
  yogurt
1 tablespoon low-calorie
  marmalade

The worst part about eating
an orange is the mess while
peeling it and the smell left
on your hands. Prepare this
dish in advance and then you
can enjoy your orange.

1. Cut the top and bottom off the orange and then remove the rest
of the peel with a sharp knife.
2. Cut into horizontal slices, remove the pips and reserve the juice.
3. Mix the yogurt and the marmalade in a small bowl and spoon
into a dish.
4. Arrange the orange slices on top and pour over any juices.

Cook's note:
This dish can be refrigerated for 2–3 hours before serving.

Variations:
Use a vanilla- or lemon-flavoured yogurt with the orange and leave
out the marmalade.
  Use raspberry or strawberry jams with the same fruit on top of
the dish.

Points per serving: 1½
Total Points per recipe: 1½

Banana Bread

Makes a 450 g (1 lb) loaf, to cut into 12 slices

Preparation time: 10 minutes
+ 1 hour cooking
Calories per slice: 185

Freezing: recommended

Ⓥ

Ripe bananas are best for this recipe, as they have a natural sweetness and mash easily.

low-fat cooking spray
200 g (7 oz) self-raising flour
1/4 teaspoon bicarbonate of soda
75 g (2³/4 oz) butter
75 g (2³/4 oz) sugar
1 tablespoon honey (optional)
 or an extra tablespoon sugar
2 eggs, beaten
2 medium ripe bananas, mashed
100 g (3¹/2 oz) sultanas (optional)

1. Spray a 450 g (1 lb) loaf tin with cooking spray. Preheat the oven to Gas Mark 4/180°C/350°F.
2. Sieve the flour and bicarbonate of soda together.
3. Cream the butter and sugar together (and the honey, if using) until light and fluffy.
4. Add the eggs gradually, beating well the whole time.
5. Stir in the flour gently but do not beat the mixture any more.
6. Stir in the mashed bananas and the sultanas, if using. Spoon into the tin and bake for about 1 hour or until just firm.
7. Turn out and cool on a rack.

Cook's note:
Wrap the loaf tightly or put it in a tin when cold and keep it for a day before slicing.

Points per slice: 3¹/2
Total Points per recipe: 43

Malt Loaf

Makes a 450 g (1 lb) loaf, to cut into 12 slices

Preparation time: 10 minutes
+ 45 minutes –1 hour cooking
Calories per slice: 105

Freezing: recommended

Ⓥ

Malt extract is available from chemist's shops. It is often used as a nutritional supplement, being high in protein and B vitamins.

225 g (8 oz) self-raising flour
25 g (1 oz) soft brown or
 granulated sugar
55 g (2 oz) sultanas
25 g (1 oz) currants
150 ml (1/4 pint) skimmed milk
1 heaped tablespoon malt extract
1 level tablespoon Golden Syrup
low-fat cooking spray

1. Preheat the oven to Gas Mark 3/170°C/325°F. Put the flour, sugar and dried fruit in a mixing bowl.
2. Warm the milk, malt extract and Golden Syrup together in a small pan, until the three have blended. If the mixture looks a little curdled, do not worry.
3. Pour the liquid into the bowl and mix together well.
4. Spray a 450 g (1 lb) loaf tin with oil.
5. Put the mixture in the tin and smooth it over with a little hot or warm water. Bake in the middle of the oven for between 45 minutes and 1 hour.
6. Leave to cool a little before turning out. When cold, wrap in foil or clingfilm. Leave for a day before slicing.

Weight Watchers note:
A very small amount of low-fat spread can be scraped over each slice but it is much better without. If you do feel the need for a spread, reduced-sugar jam (2 heaped teaspoons give 1/2 Point) would be better.

Variation:
Chopped, stoned dates can be used instead of sultanas and currants. Each date has 1/2 Point.

Points per slice: 1¹/2
Total Points per recipe: 18¹/2

Spice Scones

Makes 8 scones

Preparation time: 10 minutes
+ 10 minutes cooking
Calories per scone: 125

Freezing: recommended

Ⓥ

225 g (8 oz) self-raising flour
1 teaspoon ground mixed spice
1 teaspoon baking powder
25 g (1 oz) butter
25 g (1 oz) sugar
150 ml (1/4 pint) skimmed milk

'Quick to make and quick to bake' is a good adage for scones. They are so versatile and can be transformed with the addition of an extra flavouring (see Variations).

1. Preheat the oven to Gas Mark 8/230°C/450°F and place a baking sheet in it. Sieve the flour, spice and baking powder together into a mixing bowl.
2. Rub in the butter and then stir in the sugar. Stir in the milk and mix to a soft dough.
3. Turn out on to a floured work surface and shape into a thick round. There is no need to use a rolling pin.
4. Take the baking sheet out of the oven and put the circle of dough on it carefully. Cut into eight wedges. Put into the top of the oven and bake for 10 minutes, until brown and well risen.
5. Cool on a rack and eat while fresh, preferably on the same day.

Variations:
Add to the basic mixture as above, but without the spice or sugar, any of the following: 25 g (1 oz) grated half-fat cheese (add 1 1/2 Points to total); 1 teaspoon dried mixed herbs; 25 g (1 oz) sultanas or chopped dates (add 1 Point to total); 1 teaspoon curry powder.

Cook's notes:
If you have any sour milk, it is ideal for scones.
   While the oven is hot, use it for one or more of the baking recipes in this section. Nearly all of them can be frozen and then you will have treats in the freezer when you feel like one.

Points per scone: 2
Total Points per recipe: 17 1/2

Onion Bread

Makes a 450 g (1 lb) loaf to cut into 12 slices and 8 rolls

Preparation time: 15 minutes
+ 45 minutes cooking (bread)
or 10–15 minutes cooking
(rolls)
Calories per serving: for white
bread 90 per slice, 135 per roll;
for wholemeal bread 80 per
slice, 120 per roll

Freezing: recommended

Ⓥ

500 g (1 lb 2 oz) packaged
bread mix, either white or
wholemeal
2 tablespoons oil
2 onions, chopped
1 tablespoon chopped fresh
sage (optional)

A simple addition makes all the difference to a basic bread dough. It is delicious with soup.

1. Make up the bread mix according to the pack instructions.
2. While it is rising, heat the oil in a pan and very slowly cook the onions, without browning, for about 15 minutes. Leave on one side.
3. Preheat the oven to Gas Mark 7/220°C/425°F.
4. After the first rising, add the cooked onions to the dough and knead them in.
5. Use half the mixture to fill a 450 g (1 lb) loaf tin and the other half to make 8 round rolls (or 1 large loaf or 2 small loaves or 16 round rolls).
6. Leave for 10 minutes.
7. If using the sage, brush the top of the bread or rolls with water and sprinkle on the chopped sage.
8. Bake the rolls on the top shelf for 10–15 minutes and the bread on the bottom shelf for 45 minutes. (A large loaf will take about an hour.)
9. Remove from the tins and leave to cool on a rack.

Points per slice/per roll: 1 1/2
Total Points per recipe: 30

Index